THE

LEGAL TENDER CASES

OF 1871.

DECISION OF THE SUPREME COURT OF THE UNITED STATES, DECEMBER TERM, 1870, IN THE CASES OF KNOX *vs.* LEE, AND PARKER *vs.* DAVIS;

WITH THE OPINIONS OF

JUSTICES STRONG AND BRADLEY; AND THE DISSENTING OPINIONS OF JUSTICES CHASE, CLIFFORD, AND FIELD.

TO WHICH ARE ADDED

THE NOTES OF FORTY-FOUR CASES QUOTED OR REFERRED TO IN THE SEVERAL OPINIONS ABOVE NAMED.

New York, 1872:

PUBLISHED AT THE
OFFICE OF THE BANKERS' MAGAZINE AND STATISTICAL REGISTER.

Price, Two Dollars.

Entered according to Act of Congress, in the year 1872,

By I. SMITH HOMANS, Jr.,

In the Office of the Librarian of Congress at Washington.

STANDARD COMMERCIAL AND FINANCIAL WORKS.

EDITED BY I. SMITH HOMANS.

I. *The Cyclopedia of Commerce and Commercial Navigation*...$10 00.

The history and statistics of the staples of trade and commerce; with two thousand articles on manufactures, etc., maps and charts.

II. *A Law Manual for Bankers and Notaries*....$6 00.

Including a summary of the law and principles of commercial paper; the law of indorsement, negotiability, demand and protest, and the history of Bills of Exchange: with recent decisions of the United States Supreme Court and of the Courts of the several States in reference to Bills and Notes. To which is added a summary of the law of each State as to the rate of interest and to damages on Protested Bills of Exchange, with the latest forms of Protest and Notices of Protest.

III. *The National Currency Act*....$2 00.

Or the National Bank Act of June, 1864, with the Amendments of 1865–1870, to which are added the decisions of the Supreme Court of the United States and of the State Courts, and decisions and rulings of the Comptroller of the Currency and the Commissioner of Internal Revenue, in reference to said Act, from 1865 to 1870. This is the first and only edition comprising the entire Act, and the numerous decisions in reference thereto.

IV. *The Coin Book*....$2 50.

Comprising a History of Coinage; a Synopsis of the Mint Laws of the United States; Statistics of the Coinage from 1792 to 1870; List of Current Gold and Silver Coins, and their Custom-house Values; a Dictionary of all Coins known in Ancient and Modern Times, with their Values; the Gold and Silver Product of each State to 1870; List of Works on Coinage; the Daily Price of Gold from 1862 to 1871; with Engravings of the Principal Coins.

V. *Lawson's History of Banking*....$4 00.

With a comprehensive account of the Origin, Rise, and Progress of the Banks of England, Scotland, and Ireland. The American editor has added forty-six pages, which comprise: 1. A list of rare and useful works on banking. 2. A sketch of the origin of Savings Banks. 3. Index to articles in the English and American periodical writers on banking, coins, currency, finance, gold and silver, interest, mints, money, etc., with the names of the writers. 4. List of works on banks and currency contained in the Boston Athenæum.

VI. *The Loan and Currency Acts of the United States*....$2 00.

The United States bonds are held largely by banking institutions and by capitalists. It is highly important that the acts authorizing such issues should be in the hands of the holders of such bonds, in order that the peculiar conditions under which the several series were issued may be fully understood. The volume comprises all the acts of Congress relating to loans and the currency, from the year 1845 to 1870, both inclusive.

VII. *A History of the Bank of England*....$5 00.

Its times and traditions, from 1694 to 1844. By John Francis. With Notes, Additions, and an Appendix, including Statistics of the Bank from 1844 to 1861.

VIII. *The Banker's Common-Place Book*....$1 50.

Including contributions by A. B. Johnson and others, and a Prize Essay on Banking, or the Duties of a Young Cashier.

IX. *Bank Architecture*....$5 00.

The Merchants and Bankers' Almanac for 1868 contains engravings of twelve new designs for Banking houses, to cost from $5,000 to $75,000 each. These new Designs present a variety of fronts, adapted to village, town and city Banking institutions, with private residence for the cashier, or with offices for sub-letting; also engravings of prominent bank edifices.

THE LEGAL TENDER CASES OF 1871,

BEFORE THE SUPREME COURT OF THE UNITED STATES.

CONTENTS.

	PAG
OPINION OF THE COURT, DELIVERED BY JUSTICE STRONG	
OPINION BY JUSTICE BRADLEY	2
DISSENTING OPINION BY CHIEF JUSTICE CHASE	3
DISSENTING OPINION BY JUSTICE CLIFFORD	4
DISSENTING OPINION BY JUSTICE FIELD	8
NOTES OF CASES REFERRED TO OR QUOTED IN THE ABOVE OPINIONS	11

NOTES OF CASES

Quoted or Referred to in the Decisions of the Supreme Court of the United States in the Legal-Tender Cases of 1871.

		REPORTS.	PAGE
1.	Apsden v. Austin	5 Adolphus & Ellis	113
2.	Bank of U. S. v. Bank State of Georgia	10 Wheaton	114
3.	Bank of New York v. Supervisors	7 Wallace	114
4.	Barrington v. Potter	1 Dyer	114
5.	Briscoe v. Bank of Kentucky	8 Peters	115
6.	Bronson v. Rodes	7 Wallace	115
7.	Butler v. Horwitz	7 Wallace	115
8.	Calder v. Bull	3 Dallas	116
9.	Coffin v. Landis	10 Wright	116
10.	Cohens v. Bank of Virginia	6 Wheaton	116
11.	Collector v. Day	11 Wallace	117
12.	Commonwealth of Pennsylvania v. Smith	4 Binney	117
13.	Craig v. State of Missouri	4 Peters	118
14.	Dewing v. Sears	11 Wallace	119
15.	Dobbins v. Brown	2 Jones	119
16.	Dunn v. Sayles	5 Queen's Bench	119
17.	Faw v. Marsteller	2 Cranch	120
18.	Fisher v. United States	2 Cranch	120
19.	Fletcher v. Peck	6 Cranch	120
20.	Fox v. State of Ohio	5 Howard	121
21.	Gibbons v. Ogden	9 Wheaton	121
22.	Gwin v. Breedlove	2 Howard	121
23.	Hepburn v. Griswold	8 Wallace	122
24.	Lane County v. Oregon	7 Wallace	123
25.	Martin v. Hunter	1 Wheaton	123
26.	Metropolitan Bank v. Van Dyck	27 New York	124
27.	McCulloh v. State of Maryland	4 Wheaton	124
28.	Milligan, ex parte	4 Wallace	124
29.	Noonan v. Bradley	9 Wallace	124
30.	Ogden v. Saunders	12 Wheaton	128
31.	Peck v. Sanderson	18 Howard	128
32.	Robinson v. Noble	8 Peters	128
33.	Sibbald v. United States	12 Peters	129
34.	Snow v. Perry	9 Pickering	129
35.	State of Texas v. White	7 Wallace	130
36.	Sturges v. Crowninshield	4 Wheaton	131
37.	Thorndike v. United States	2 Mason	132
38.	Thompson v. Riggs	5 Wallace	133
39.	United States v. Marigold	9 Howard	133
40.	Veazie Bank v. Fenno	8 Wallace	134
41.	Ward v. State of Maryland	12 Wallace	134
42.	Washington Bridge Co. v. Stewart	3 Howard	135
43.	Workman v. Mifflin	6 Casey	136
44.	Willard v. Tayloe	8 Wallace	136
45.	Wright v. Reid	3 Term Reports	137

One Volume, Octavo. Published at the Office of the Bankers' Magazine, New York.

THE LEGAL TENDER CASES.

Before the Supreme Court of the United States,

December Term, 1870.

The case of WILLIAM B. KNOX, *Plaintiff in Error, vs.* PHŒBE G. LEE *and* HUGH LEE, *her husband. In Error to the Circuit Court of the United States for the Western District of* TEXAS, *and*

THOMAS H. PARKER *Plaintiff in Error, vs.* GEORGE DAVIS. *In error to the Supreme Judicial Court of the Commonwealth of* MASSACHUSETTS.

Mr. Justice STRONG delivered the opinion of the Court.

The controlling questions in these cases are the following: Are the acts of Congress, known as the legal-tender acts, constitutional when applied to contracts made before their passage; and, secondly, are they valid as applicable to debts contracted since their enactment? These questions have been elaborately argued, and they have received from the court that consideration which their great importance demands. It would be difficult to over-estimate the consequences which must follow our decision. They will affect the entire business of the country, and take hold of the possible continued existence of the government. If it be held by this court that Congress has no constitutional power, under any circumstances, or in any emergency, to make treasury notes a legal tender for the payment of all debts, (a power confessedly possessed by every independent sovereignty other than the United States,) the government is without those means of self-preservation which, all must admit, may, in certain contingencies, become indispensable, even if they were not when the acts of Congress now called in question were enacted. It is also clear that if we hold the acts invalid as applicable to debts incurred, or transactions which have taken place since their enactment, our decision must cause, throughout the country, great business derangement, wide-spread distress, and the rankest injustice. The debts which have been contracted since February 25, 1862, constitute, doubtless, by far the greatest portion of the existing indebtedness of the country. They have been contracted in view of the acts of Congress declaring treasury notes a legal tender, and in reliance upon that declaration. Men have bought and sold, borrowed and lent, and assumed every variety of obligations contemplating that payment might be made with such notes. Indeed, legal-tender treasury notes have become the universal measure of values.

If now, by our decision, it be established that these debts and obligations can be discharged only by gold coin ; if, contrary to the expectation of all parties to these contracts, legal-tender notes are rendered unavailable, the government has become an instrument of the grossest injustice ; all debtors are loaded with an obligation it was never contemplated they should assume ; a large percentage is added to every debt, and such must become the demand for gold to satisfy contracts, that ruinous sacrifices, general distress, and bankruptcy may be expected. These consequences are too obvious to admit of question. And there is no well-founded distinction to be made between the constitutional validity of an act of Congress declaring treasury notes a legal tender for the payment of debts contracted after its passage and that of an act making them a legal tender for the discharge of all debts, as well those incurred before as those made after its enactment. There may be a difference in the effects produced by the acts, and in the hardship of their operation, but in both cases the fundamental question, that which tests the validity of the legislation, is, can Congress constitutionally give to treasury notes the character and qualities of money? Can such notes be constituted a legitimate circulating medium, having a defined legal value? If they can, then such notes must be available to fulfill all contracts (not expressly excepted) solvable in money, without reference to the time when the contracts were made. Hence it is not strange that those who hold the legal-tender acts unconstitutional when applied to contracts made before February, 1862, find themselves compelled also to hold that the acts are invalid as to debts created after that time, and to hold that both classes of debts alike can be discharged only by gold and silver coin.

The consequences of which we have spoken, serious as they are, must be accepted, if there is a clear incompatibility between the Constitution and the legal-tender acts. But we are unwilling to precipitate them upon the country, unless such an incompatibility plainly appears. A decent respect for a co-ordinate branch of the government demands that the judiciary should presume, until the contrary is clearly shown, that there has been no transgression of power by Congress—all the members of which act under the obligation of an oath of fidelity to the Constitution. Such has always been the rule. In COMMONWEALTH *vs.* SMITH, (4 *Binney*, 123,) the language of the court was, " it must be remembered that, for weighty reasons, it has been assumed as a principle, in construing constitutions by the Supreme Court of the United States, by this court, and by every other court of reputation in the United States, that an act of the legislature is not to be declared void unless the violation of the Constitution is so manifest as to leave no room for reasonable doubt ;" and, in FLETCHER *vs.* PECK, (6 *Cranch,* 87,) Chief Justice MARSHALL said " it is not on slight implication and vague conjecture that the legislature is to be pronounced to have transcended its powers and its acts to be considered void. The opposition between the Constitution and the law should be such that the judge feels a clear and strong conviction of their incompatibility with each other." It is incumbent, there fore, upon those who affirm the unconstitutionality of an act of Congress to show clearly that it is in violation of the provisions of the Constitution. It is not sufficient for them that they succeed in raising a doubt.

Nor can it be questioned that, when investigating the nature and extent of the powers conferred by the Constitution upon Congress, it is indispensable to keep in view the objects for which those powers were granted. This is an universal rule of construction applied alike to statutes, wills, contracts, and constitutions. If the general purpose of the instrument is ascertained, the language of its provisions must be construed with reference to that purpose and so as to subserve it. In no other way can the intent of the framers of the instrument be discovered. And there are more urgent reasons for looking to the ultimate purpose in examining the powers conferred by a constitution than there are in construing a statute, a will, or a contract. We do not expect to find in a constitution minute details. It is necessarily brief and comprehensive. It prescribes outlines, leaving the filling up to be deduced from the outlines. In MARTIN *vs*. HUNTER, 1 *Wheaton*, 326, it was said, "the Constitution unavoidably deals in general language. It did not suit the purpose of the people in framing this great charter of our liberties to provide for minute specifications of its powers, or to declare the means by which those powers should be carried into execution."

And with singular clearness was it said by Chief Justice MARSHALL, in McCULLOH *vs*. THE STATE OF MARYLAND, 4 *Wheaton*, 405 : " A constitution, to contain an accurate detail of all the subdivisions of which its great powers will admit, and of all the means by which it may be carried into execution, would partake of the prolixity of a political code, and would scarcely be embraced by the human mind. It would probably never be understood by the public. Its nature, therefore, requires that only its great outlines should be marked, its important objects designated, and the minor ingredients which compose those objects be deduced from the nature of the objects themselves." If these are correct principles, if they are proper views of the manner in which the Constitution is to be understood, the powers conferred upon Congress must be regarded as related to each other, and all means for a common end. Each is but part of a system, a constituent of one whole. No single power is the ultimate end for which the Constitution was adopted. It may, in a very proper sense, be treated as a means for the accomplishment of a subordinate object, but that object is itself a means designed for an ulterior purpose. Thus the power to levy and collect taxes, to coin money and regulate its value, to raise and support armies, or to provide for and maintain a navy, are instruments for the paramount object, which was to establish a government, sovereign within its sphere, with capability of self-preservation, thereby forming an union more perfect than that which existed under the old Confederacy.

The same may be asserted also of all the non-enumerated powers included in the authority expressly given " to make all laws which shall be necessary and proper for carrying into execution the specified powers vested in Congress, and all other powers vested by the Constitution in the government of the United States, or in any department or officer thereof." It is impossible to know what those non-enumerated powers are, and what is their nature and extent, without considering the purposes they were intended to subserve. Those purposes, it must be noted, reach beyond the mere execution of all powers definitely entrusted to Congress, and mentioned in detail. They embrace the execution of all other powers vested by the Constitution in the government of the United States, or in any department or officer thereof. It certainly was intended to confer upon the government the power of self-preservation. Said Chief Justice MARSHALL, in COHENS vs. THE BANK OF VIRGINIA, 6 *Wheaton*, 414 : "America has chosen to be, in many respects and to many purposes, a nation, and for all these purposes her government is complete; for all these objects it is supreme. It can then, in effecting these objects, legitimately control all individuals or governments within the American territory." He added, in the same case : " A constitution is framed for ages to come, and is designed to approach immortality as near as mortality can approach it. Its course cannot always be tranquil. It is exposed to storms and tempests, and its framers must be unwise statesmen, indeed, if they have not provided it, as far as its nature will permit, with the means of self-preservation from the perils it is sure to encounter." That would appear, then, to be a most unreasonable construction of the Constitution which denies to the government created by it, the right to employ freely every means, not prohibited, necessary for its preservation, and for the fulfillment of its acknowledged duties. Such a right, we hold, was given by the last clause of the eighth section of its first article. The means or instrumentalities referred to in that clause, and authorized, are not enumerated or defined. In the nature of things enumeration and specification were impossible. But they were left to the discretion of Congress, subject only to the restrictions that they be not prohibited, and be necessary and proper for carrying into execution the enumerated powers given to Congress, and all other powers vested in the government of the United States, or in any department or officer thereof.

And here it is to be observed it is not indispensable to the existence of any power claimed for the federal government that it can be found specified in the words of the Constitution, or clearly and directly traceable to some one of the specified powers. Its existence may be deduced fairly from more than one of the substantive powers expressly defined, or from them all combined. It is allowable to group together any number of them and infer from them all that the power claimed has been conferred. Such a treatment of the Constitution is recognized by its own provisions. This is well illustrated in its language respecting the writ of habeas corpus. The power to suspend the privilege of that writ is not expressly given, nor can it be deduced from any one of the particularized grants of power. Yet it is provided that the privileges of the writ shall not be suspended except in certain defined contingencies. This is no express grant of power. It is a restriction. But it shows irresistibly that somewhere in the Constitution power to suspend the privilege of the writ was granted, either by some one or more of the specifications of power, or by them all combined. And, that important powers were understood by the people who adopted the Constitution to have been created by it, powers not enumerated, and not included incidentally in any one of those enumerated, is shown by the amendments. The first ten of these were suggested in the conventions of the states, and proposed at the first session of the first Congress, before any complaint was made of a disposition to assume doubtful powers. The preamble to the resolution submitting them for adoption recited that the "conventions of a number of the states had, at the time of their adopting the Constitution, expressed a desire, in order to prevent misconstruction or abuse of its powers, that further declaratory and *restrictive* clauses should be added." This was the origin of the amendments, and they are significant. They tend plainly to show that, in the judgment of those who adopted the Constitution, there were powers created by it, neither expressly specified nor deducible from any one specified power, or ancillary to it alone, but which grew out of the aggregate of powers conferred upon the government, or out of the sovereignty instituted. Most of these amendments are denials of power which had not been expressly granted, and which cannot be said to have been necessary and proper for carrying into execution any other powers. Such, for example, is the prohibition of any laws respecting the establishment of religion, prohibiting the free exercise thereof, or abridging the freedom of speech or of the press.

And it is of importance to observe that Congress has often exercised, without question, powers that are not expressly given nor ancillary to any single enumerated power. Powers thus exercised are what are called by Judge STORY, in his Commentaries on the Constitution, resulting powers, arising from the aggregate powers of the government. He instances the right to sue and make contracts. Many others might be given. The oath required by law from officers of the government is one. So is building a capitol or a presidential mansion, and so also is the penal code. This last is worthy of brief notice. Congress is expressly authorized "to provide for the punishment of counterfeiting the securities and current coin of the United States, and to define and punish piracies and felonies committed on the high seas and offences against the laws of nations." It is also empowered to declare the punishment of treason, and provision is made for impeachments. This is the extent of power to punish crime expressly conferred. It might be argued that the expression of these limited powers implies an exclusion of all other subjects of criminal legislation. Such is the argument in the present cases. It is said because Congress is authorized to coin money and regulate its value it cannot declare any thing other than gold and silver to be money or make it a legal tender. Yet Congress, by the act of April 30, 1790, entitled "An act more effectually to provide for the punishment of certain crimes against the United States," and the supplementary act of March 3d, 1825, defined and provided for the punishment of a large class of crimes other than those mentioned in the Constitution, and some of the punishments prescribed are manifestly not in aid of any single substantive power. No one doubts that this was rightfully done, and the power thus exercised has been affirmed by this court.—(UNITED STATES *vs.* MARIGOLD, 9 *Howard,* 560.) This case shows that a power may exist as an aid to the execution of an express power, on an aggregate of such powers, though there is another express power given relating in part to the same subject, but less extensive. Another illustration of this may be found in connection with the provisions respecting a census. The Constitution orders an enumeration of free persons in the different states every ten years. The direction extends no further. Yet Congress has repeatedly directed an enumeration not only of free persons in the states, but of free persons in the territories ; and not only an enumeration of persons, but the collection of statistics respecting age, sex, and production. Who questions the power to do this ?

Indeed, the whole history of the government and of congressional legislation has exhibited the use of a very wide discretion, even in times of peace and in the absence of any trying emergency, in the selection of the necessary and proper means to carry into effect the great objects for which the government was framed, and this discretion has generally been unquestioned, or, if questioned, sanctioned by this court. This is true not only when an attempt has been made to execute a single power specifically given, but equally true when the means adopted have been appropriate to the execution, not of a single authority, but of all the powers created by the Constitution. Under the power to establish post-offices and post-roads Congress has provided for carrying the mails, punishing theft of letters and mail robberies, and even for transporting the mails to foreign countries. Under the power to regulate commerce provision has been made by law for the improvement of harbors, the establishment of observatories, the erection of light-houses, break-waters, and buoys, the registry, enrolment, and construction of ships, and a code has been enacted for the government of seamen. Under the same power and other powers over the revenue and the currency of the country, for the convenience of the treasury and internal commerce, a corporation known as the United States Bank was early created. To its capital the government subscribed one-fifth of its stock. But the corporation was a private one, doing business for its own profit. Its incorporation was a constitutional exercise of congressional power for no other reason than that it was deemed to be a convenient instrument or means for accomplishing one or more of the ends for which the government was established, or, in the language of the first article, already quoted, " necessary and proper " for carrying into execution some or all the powers vested in the government. Clearly, this necessity, if any existed, was not a direct and obvious one. Yet this court, in MCCULLOH *vs.* THE STATE OF MARYLAND, 4 *Wheaton,* 416, unanimously ruled that in authorizing the bank Congress had not transcended its powers. So debts due to the United States have been declared by acts of Congress entitled to priority of payment over debts due to other creditors, and this court has held such acts warranted by the Constitution.—(FISHER *vs.* BLIGHT, 2 *Cranch,* 358.)

generally, which threatened loss of confidence in the ability of the government to maintain its continued existence, and therewith the complete destruction of all remaining national credit.

It was at such a time and in such circumstances that Congress was called upon to devise means for maintaining the army and navy, for securing the large supplies of money needed, and, indeed, for the preservation of the government created by the Constitution. It was at such a time and in such an emergency that the legal-tender acts were passed. Now, if it were certain that nothing else would have supplied the absolute necessities of the treasury, that nothing else would have enabled the government to maintain its armies and navy, that nothing else would have saved the government and the Constitution from destruction, while the legal-tender acts would, could any one be bold enough to assert that Congress transgressed its powers? Or if these enactments did work these results, can it be maintained now that they were not for a legitimate end, or "appropriate and adapted to that end," in the language of Chief Justice MARSHALL? That they did work such results is not to be doubted. Something revived the drooping faith of the people; something brought immediately to the government's aid the resources of the nation; and something enabled the successful prosecution of the war, and the preservation of national life. What was it, if not the legal-tender enactments?

But if it be conceded that some other means might have been chosen for the accomplishment of these legitimate and necessary ends, the concession does not weaken the argument. It is urged now, after the lapse of nine years, and when the emergency has passed, that treasury notes without the legal-tender clause might have been issued, and that the necessities of the government might thus have been supplied. Hence it is inferred there was no necessity for giving to the notes issued the capability of paying private debts. At best this is mere conjecture. But admitting it be true, what does it prove? Nothing more than that Congress had the choice of means for a legitimate end, each appropriate, and adapted to that end, though, perhaps, in different degrees. What then? Can this court say that it ought to have adopted one rather than the other? Is it our province to decide that the means selected were beyond the constitutional power of Congress, because we may think that other means to the same ends would have been more appropriate and equally efficient? That would be to assume legislative power, and to disregard the accepted rules for construing the Constitution. The degree of the necessity for any congressional enactment, or the relative degree of its appropriateness, if it have any appropriateness, is for consideration in Congress, not here. Said Chief Justice MARSHALL, in McCULLOH *vs.* MARYLAND, as already stated, "When the law is not prohibited, and is really calculated to effect any of the objects entrusted to the government, to undertake here to inquire into the degree of this necessity, would be to pass the line which circumscribes the judicial department, and to tread on legislative ground."

It is plain to our view, however, that none of those measures which it is now conjectured might have been substituted for the legal-tender acts could have met the exigencies of the case, at the time when those acts were passed. We have said that the credit of the government had been tried to its utmost endurance. Every new issue of notes which had nothing more to rest on than government credit, must have paralyzed it more and more, and rendered it increasingly difficult to keep the army in the field, or the navy afloat. It is an historical fact that many persons and institutions refused to receive and pay those notes that had been issued, and even the head of the treasury represented to Congress the necessity of making the new issues legal tenders, or rather, declared it impossible to avoid the necessity. The vast body of men in the military service was composed of citizens who had left their farms, their workshops, and their business, with families and debts to be provided for. The government could not pay them with ordinary treasury notes, nor could they discharge their debts with such a currency. Something more was needed—something that had all the uses of money. And as no one could be compelled to take common treasury notes in payment of debts, and as the prospect of ultimate redemption was remote and contingent, it is not too much to say that they must have depreciated in the market long before the war closed, as did the currency of the Confederate States. Making the notes legal tenders, gave them a new use, and it needs no argument to show that the value of things is in proportion to the uses to which they may be applied.

It may be conceded that Congress is not authorized to enact laws in furtherance even of a legitimate end, merely because they are useful, or because they make the government stronger. There must be some relation between the means and the end; some adaptedness or appropriateness of the laws to carry into execution the powers created by the Constitution. But when a statute has proved effective in the execution of powers confessedly existing, it is not too much to say that it must have had some appropriateness to the execution of those powers. The rules of construction heretofore adopted do not demand that the relationship between the means and the end shall be direct and immediate. Illustrations of this may be found in several of the cases above cited. The charter of a bank of the United States, the priority given to debts due the government over private debts, and the exemption of federal loans from liability to state taxation, are only a few of the many which might be given. The case of VEAZIE BANK *vs.* FENNO, 8 *Wallace*, 533, presents a suggestive illustration. There a tax of ten per cent. on state bank notes in circulation was held constitutional, not merely because it was a means of raising revenue, but as an instrument to put out of existence such a circulation in competition with notes issued by the government. There, this court, speaking through the Chief Justice, avowed that it is the constitutional right of Congress to provide a currency for the whole country; that this might be done by coin, or United States notes, or notes of National Banks; and that it cannot be questioned Congress may constitutionally secure the benefit of such a currency to the people by appropriate legislation. It was said there can be no question of the power of this government to emit bills of credit; to make them receivable in payment of debts to itself; to fit them for use by those who see fit to use them in all the transactions of commerce; to make them a currency uniform in value and description, and convenient and useful for circulation. Here the substantive power to tax was allowed to be employed for improving the currency. It is not easy to see why, if state bank notes can be taxed out of existence for the purposes of indirectly making United States notes more convenient and useful for commercial purposes, the same end may not be secured directly by making them a legal tender.

Concluding, then, that the provision which made treasury notes a legal tender for the payment of all debts other than those expressly excepted, was not an inappropriate means for carrying into execution the legitimate powers of the government, we proceed to inquire whether it was forbidden by the letter or spirit of the Constitution. It is not claimed that any express prohibition exists, but it is insisted that the spirit of the Constitution was violated by the enactment. Here those who assert the unconstitutionality of the acts mainly rest their argument. They claim that the clause which conferred upon Congress power " to coin money, regulate the value thereof, and of foreign coin," contains an implication that nothing but that which is the subject of coinage, nothing but the precious metals, can ever be declared by law to be money, or to have the uses of money. If by this is meant that because certain powers over the currency are expressly given to Congress, all other powers relating to the same subject are impliedly forbidden, we need only remark that such is not the manner in which the Constitution has always been construed. On the contrary, it has been ruled that power over a particular subject may be exercised as auxiliary to an express power, though there is another express power relating to the same subject, less comprehensive.—(U. S. *vs.* MARIGOLD, 9 *Howard,* 560.) There an express power to punish a certain class of crimes (the only direct reference to criminal legislation contained in the Constitution,) was not regarded as an objection to deducing authority to punish other crimes from another substantive and defined grant of power. There are other decisions to the same effect. To assert, then, that the clause enabling Congress to coin money and regulate its value tacitly implies a denial of all other power over the currency of the nation, is an attempt to introduce a new rule of construction against the solemn decisions of this court. So far from its containing a lurking prohibition, many have thought it was intended to confer upon Congress that general power over the currency which has always been an acknowledged attribute of sovereignty in every other civilized nation than our own, especially when considered in connection with the other clause which denies to the states the power to coin money, emit bills of credit, or make any thing but gold and silver coin a tender in payment of debts.

We do not assert this now, but there are some considerations touching these clauses which tend to show that if any implications are to be deduced from them, they are of an enlarging rather than a restraining character. The Constitution was intended to frame a government as distinguished from a league or compact, a government supreme in some particulars over states and people. It was designed to provide the same currency, having an uniform legal value in all the states. It was for this reason the power to coin money and regulate its value was conferred upon the federal government, while the same power as well as the power to emit bills of credit was withdrawn from the states. The states can no longer declare what shall be money, or regulate its value. Whatever power there is over the currency is vested in Congress. If the power to declare what is money is not in Congress, it is annihilated. This may indeed have been intended. Some powers that usually belong to sovereignties were extinguished, but their extinguishment was not left to inference. In most cases, if not in all, when it was intended that governmental powers, commonly acknowledged as such, should cease to exist, both in the states and in the federal government, it was expressly denied to both, as well to the United States as to the individual states. And generally, when one of such powers was expressly denied to the states only, it was for the purpose of rendering the federal power more complete and exclusive. Why, then, it may be asked, if the design was to prohibit to the new government, as well as to the states, that general power over the currency which the states had when the Constitution was framed, was such denial not expressly extended to the new government, as it was to the states? In view of this, it might be argued with much force that when it is considered in what brief and comprehensive terms the Constitution speaks, how sensible its framers must have been that emergencies might arise when the precious metals (then more scarce than now) might prove inadequate to the necessities of the government and the demands of the people—when it is remembered that paper money was almost exclusively in use in the states as the medium of exchange, and when the great evil sought to be remedied was the want of uniformity in the current value of money, it might be argued, we say, that the gift of power to coin money and regulate the value thereof, was understood as conveying general power over the currency, the power which had belonged to the states, and which they surrendered. Such a construction, it might be said, would be in close analogy to the mode of construing other substantive powers granted to Congress. They have never been construed literally, and the government could not exist if they were. Thus the power to carry on war is conferred by the power to "declare war."

The whole system of the transportation of the mails is built upon the power to establish post-offices and post-roads. The power to regulate commerce has also been extended far beyond the letter of the grant. Even the advocates of a strict literal construction of the phrase, "to coin money and regulate the value thereof," while insisting that it defines the material to be coined as metal, are compelled to concede to Congress large discretion in all other particulars. The Constitution does not ordain what metals may be coined, or prescribe that the legal value of the metals, when coined, shall correspond at all with their intrinsic value in the market. Nor does it even affirm that Congress may declare anything to be a legal tender for the payment of debts. Confessedly, the power to regulate the value of money coined, and of foreign coins, is not exhausted by the first regulation. More than once in our history has the regulation been changed without any denial of the power of Congress to change it, and it seems to have been left to Congress to determine alike what metal shall be coined, its purity, and how far its statutory value, as money, shall correspond, from time to time, with the market value of the same metal as bullion. How, then, can the grant of a power to coin money and regulate its value, made in terms so liberal and unrestrained, coupled also with a denial to the states of all power over the currency, be regarded as an implied prohibition to Congress against declaring treasury notes a legal tender, if such a declaration is appropriate, and adapted to carrying into execution the admitted powers of the government?

We do not, however, rest our assertion of the power of Congress to enact legal-tender laws upon this grant. We assert only that the grant can, in no just sense, be regarded as containing an implied prohibition against their enactment, and that, if it raises any implications, they are of complete power over the currency, rather than restraining.

We come next to the argument much used, and, indeed, the main reliance of those who assert the unconstitutionality of the legal-tender acts. It is that they are prohibited by the spirit of the Constitution because they indirectly impair the obligation of contracts. The argument, of course, relates only to those contracts which were made before February, 1862, when the first act was passed, and it has no bearing upon the question whether the acts are valid when applied to contracts made after their passage. The argument assumes two things—*first*, that the acts do, in effect, impair the obligation of contracts, and, *second*, that Congress is prohibited from taking any action which may indirectly have that effect. Neither of these assumptions can be accepted. It is true, that under the acts, a debtor who became such before they were passed, may discharge his debt with the notes authorized by them, and the creditor is compellable to receive such notes in discharge of his claim. But whether the obligation of the contract is thereby weakened can be determined only after considering what was the contract obligation. It was not a duty to pay gold or silver, or the kind of money recognized by law at the time when the contract was made, nor was it a duty to pay money of equal intrinsic value in the market. (We speak now of contracts to pay money generally, not contracts to pay some specifically defined species of money.) The expectation of the creditor and the anticipation of the debtor may have been that the contract would be discharged by the payment of coined metals, but neither the expectation of one party to the contract respecting its fruits, nor the anticipation of the other constitutes its obligation. There is a well recognized distinction between the expectation of the parties to a contract, and the duty imposed by it.—(APSDEN *vs.* AUSTIN, 5 *Adolphus & Ellis, N.S.*, 671; DUNN *vs.* SAYLES, *Ibid.*, 685; COFFIN *vs.* LANDIS, 10 *Wright*, 426.) Were it not so, the expectation of results would be always equivalent to a binding engagement that they should follow. But the *obligation* of a contract to pay money is to pay that which the law shall recognize as money when the payment is to be made. If there is any thing settled by decision it is this, and we do not understand it to be controverted.—(*Davies' Reps.*, 28; BARRINGTON *vs.* POTTER, *Dyer*, 81, b., fol. 67; FAW *vs.* MARSTELLER, 2 *Cranch*, 29.) No one ever doubted that a debt of one thousand dollars, contracted before 1834, could be paid by one hundred eagles coined after that year, though they contained no more gold than ninety-four eagles, such as were coined when the contract was made, and this, not because of the intrinsic value of the coin, but because of its legal value. The eagles coined after 1834 were not money until they were authorized by law; and had they been coined before, without a law fixing their legal value, they could no more have paid a debt than uncoined bullion, or cotton, or wheat. Every contract for the payment of money, simply, is necessarily subject to the constitutional power of the government over the currency, whatever that power may be, and the obligation of the parties is, therefore, assumed with reference to that power. Nor is this singular. A covenant of quiet enjoyment is not broken, nor is its obligation impaired by the government's taking the land granted in virtue of its right of eminent domain. The expectation of the covenantee may be disappointed. He may not enjoy all he anticipated, but the grant was made and the covenant undertaken in subordination to the paramount right of the government.—(DOBBINS *vs.* BROWN, 2 *Jones*, 75; WORKMAN *vs.* MIFFLIN, 6 *Casey*, 362.) We have been asked whether Congress can declare that a contract to deliver a quantity of grain may be satisfied by the tender of a less quantity. Undoubtedly not. But this is a false analogy. There is a wide distinction between a tender of quantities, or of specific articles, and a tender of legal values. Contracts for the delivery of specific articles belong exclusively to the domain of state legislation, while contracts for the payment of money are subject to the authority of Congress, at least so far as relates to the means of payment. They are engagements to pay with lawful money of the United States, and Congress is empowered to regulate that money. It cannot, therefore be maintained that the legal-tender acts impaired the obligation of contracts.

Nor can it be truly asserted that Congress may not, by its action, indirectly impair the obligation of contracts, if by the expression be meant rendering contracts fruitless, or partially fruitless. Directly it may, confessedly, by passing a bankrupt act, embracing past as well as future transactions. This is obliterating contracts entirely. So it may relieve parties from their apparent obligations indirectly in a multitude of ways. It may declare war, or, even in peace, pass non-intercourse acts, or direct an embargo. All such measures may, and must operate seriously upon existing contracts, and may not merely hinder, but relieve the parties to such contracts entirely from performance. It is, then, clear that the powers of Congress may be exerted, though the effect of such exertion may be in one case to annul, and in other cases to impair the obligation of contracts. And it is no sufficient answer to this to say it is true only when the powers exerted were expressly granted. There is no ground for any such distinction. It has no warrant in the Constitution, or in any of the decisions of this court. We are accustomed to speak for mere convenience of the express and implied powers conferred upon Congress. But, in fact, the auxiliary powers, those necessary and appropriate to the execution of other powers singly described, are as expressly given as is the power to declare war, or to establish uniform laws on the subject of bankruptcy. They are not catalogued, no list of them is made, but they are grouped in the last clause of section eight of the first article, and granted in the same words in which all other powers are granted to Congress. And this court has recognized no such distinction as is now attempted. An embargo suspends many contracts and renders performance of others impossible, yet the power to enforce it has been declared constitutional.—(GIBBONS vs. OGDEN, 9 Wheaton, 1.) The power to enact a law directing an embargo is one of the auxiliary powers, existing only because appropriate in time of peace to regulate commerce, or appropriate to carrying on war. Though not conferred as a substantive power, it has not been thought to be in conflict with the Constitution, because it impairs indirectly the obligation of contracts. That discovery calls for a new reading of the Constitution.

If, then, the legal-tender acts were justly chargeable with impairing contract obligations, they would not, for that reason, be forbidden, unless a different rule is to be applied to them from that which has hitherto prevailed in the construction of other powers granted by the fundamental law. But, as already intimated, the objection misapprehends the nature and extent of the contract obligation spoken of in the Constitution. As in a state of civil society property of a citizen or subject is ownership, subject to the lawful demands of the sovereign, so contracts must be understood as made in reference to the possible exercise of the rightful authority of the government, and no obligation of a contract can extend to the defeat of legitimate government authority.

Closely allied to the objection we have just been considering is the argument pressed upon us that the legal-tender acts were prohibited by the spirit of the fifth amendment, which forbids taking private property for public use without just compensation or due process of law. That provision has always been understood as referring only to a direct appropriation, and not to consequential injuries resulting from the exercise of lawful power. It has never been supposed to have any bearing upon, or to inhibit laws that indirectly work harm and loss to individuals. A new tariff, an embargo, a draft, or a war may inevitably bring upon individuals great losses; may, indeed, render valuable property almost valueless. They may destroy the worth of contracts. But who ever supposed that, because of this, a tariff could not be changed, or a non-intercourse act, or an embargo be enacted, or a war be declared? By the act of June 28, 1834, a new regulation of the weight and value of gold coin was adopted, and about six per cent. was taken from the weight of each dollar. The effect of this was that all creditors were subjected to a corresponding loss. The debts then due became solvable with six per cent. less gold than was required to pay them before. The result was thus precisely what it is contended the legal-tender acts worked. But was it ever imagined this was taking private property without compensation or without due process of law? Was the idea ever advanced that the new regulation of gold coin was against the spirit of the fifth amendment? And has any one in good faith avowed his belief that even a law debasing the current coin, by increasing the alloy, would be taking private property? It might be impolitic and unjust, but could its constitutionality be doubted? Other statutes have, from time to time, reduced the quantity of silver in silver coin without any question of their constitutionality. It is said, however, now, that the act of 1834 only brought the legal value of gold coin more nearly into correspondence with its actual value in the market, or its relative value to silver. But we do not perceive that this varies the case or diminishes its force as an illustration. The creditor who had a thousand dollars due him on the 31st day of July, 1834, (the day before the act took effect) was entitled to a thousand dollars of coined gold of the weight and fineness of the then existing coinage. The day after he was entitled only to a sum six per cent. less in weight and in market value, or to a smaller number of silver dollars. Yet he would have been a bold man who had asserted that, because of this, the obligation of the contract was impaired, or that private property was taken without compensation or without due process of law. No such assertion, so far as we know, was ever made. Admit it was a hardship, but it is not every hardship that is unjust, much less that is unconstitutional; and certainly it would be an anomaly for us to hold an act of Congress invalid merely because we might think its provisions harsh and unjust.

We are not aware of anything else which has been advanced in support of the proposition that the legal-tender acts were forbidden by either the letter or the spirit of the Constitution. If, therefore, they were, what we have endeavored to show, appropriate means for legitimate ends, they were not transgressive of the authority vested in Congress.

Here we might stop; but we will notice briefly an argument presented in support of the position that the unit of money value must possess intrinsic value. The argument is derived from assimilating the constitutional provision respecting a standard of weights and measures to that confering the power to coin money and regulate its value. It is said there can be no uniform standard of weights without weight, or of measure without length or space, and we are asked how any thing can be made an uniform standard of value which has itself no value? This is a question foreign to the subject before us. The legal-tender acts do not attempt to make paper a standard of value. We do not rest their validity upon the assertion that their emission is coinage, or any regulation of the value of money; nor do we assert that Congress may make anything which has no value money. What we do assert is, that Congress has power to enact that the government's promises to pay money shall be, for the time being, equivalent in value to the representative of value determined by the coinage acts, or to multiples thereof. It is hardly correct to speak of a standard of value. The Constitution does not speak of it. It contemplates a standard for that which has gravity or extension; but value is an ideal thing. The coinage acts fix its unit as a dollar; but the gold or silver thing we call a dollar is, in no sense, a standard of a dollar. It is a representative of it. There might never have been a piece of money of the denomination of a dollar. There never was a pound sterling coined until 1815, if we except a few coins struck in the reign of Henry VIII., almost immediately debased, yet it has been the unit of British currency for many generations. It is, then, a mistake to regard the legal-tender acts as either fixing a standard of value or regulating money values, or making that money which has no intrinsic value.

But, without extending our remarks further, it will be seen that we hold the acts of Congress constitutional as applied to contracts made either before or after their passage. In so holding we overrule so much of what was decided in HEPBURN *vs.* GRISWOLD, (8 *Wallace*, 603,) as ruled the acts unwarranted by the Constitution so far as they apply to contracts made before their enactment. That case was decided by a divided court, and by a court having a less number of judges than the law then in existence provided this court shall have. These cases have been heard before a full court, and they have received our most careful consideration. The questions involved are constitutional questions of the most vital importance to the government and to the public at large. We have been in the habit of treating cases involving a consideration of constitutional power differently from those which concern merely private right.—(BRISCOE *vs.* BANK OF KENTUCKY, 8 *Peters*, 118.) We are not accustomed to hear them in the absence of a full court, if it can be avoided. Even in cases involving only private rights, if convinced we had made a mistake, we would hear another argument and correct our error. And it is no unprecedented thing in courts of last resort, both in this country and in England, to overrule decisions previously made. We agree this should not be done inconsiderately, but in a case of such far-reaching consequences as the present, thoroughly convinced as we are that Congress has not transgressed its powers, we regard it as our duty so to decide and to affirm both these judgments.

The other questions raised in the case of William B. Knox against Phœbe Lee and Hugh Lee were substantially decided in TEXAS *vs* WHITE (7 *Wallace*, 700).

The judgment in each case is affirmed.

OPINION BY MR. JUSTICE BRADLEY.

Before the Supreme Court of the United States,

December Term, 1870.

The cases of WILLIAM B. KNOX, *Plaintiff in Error, vs.* PHŒBE G. LEE *and* HUGH LEE, *her husband. In Error to the Circuit Court of the United States for the Western District of* TEXAS, *and*

THOMAS H. PARKER, *Plaintiff in Error, vs.* GEORGE DAVIS. *In error to the Supreme Judicial Court of the Commonwealth of* MASSACHUSETTS.

I concur in the opinion just read, and should feel that it was out of place to add anything further on the subject were it not for its great importance. On a constitutional question involving the powers of the government it is proper that every aspect of it, and every consideration bearing upon it, should be presented, and that no member of the court should hesitate to express his views. I do not propose, however, to go into the subject at large, but only to make such additional observations as appear to me proper for consideration, at the risk of some inadvertent repetition.

The Constitution of the United States established a government, and not a league, compact, or partnership. It was constituted by the people. It is called a government. In the eighth section of article I. it is declared that Congress shall have power to make all laws which shall be necessary and proper for carrying into execution the foregoing powers, and all other powers vested by this Constitution in *the government of the United States,* or in any department or office thereof. As a government it was invested with all the attributes of sovereignty. It is expressly declared in article VI. that the Constitution, and the laws of the United States made in pursuance thereof, and all treaties made under the authority of the United States, shall be the supreme law of the land.

The doctrine so long contended for, that the federal Union was a mere compact of states, and that the states, if they chose, might annul or disregard the acts of the national legislature, or might secede from the Union at their pleasure, and that the general government had no power to coerce them into submission to the Constitution, should be regarded as definitely and forever overthrown. This has been finally effected by the national power, as it had often been before, by overwhelming argument.

The United States is not only a government, but it is a national government, and the only government in this country that has the character of nationality. It is invested with power over all the foreign relations of the country, war, peace, and negotiations and intercourse with other nations; all which is forbidden to the state governments. It has jurisdiction over all those general subjects of legislation and sovereignty which affect the interests of the whole people equally and alike, and which require uniformity of regulations and laws, such as the coinage, weights and measures, bankruptcies, the postal system, patent and copyright laws, the public lands, and inter-state commerce; all which subjects are expressly or impliedly prohibited to the State governments. It has power to suppress insurrections, as well as to repel invasions, and to organize, arm, discipline, and call into service the militia of the whole country. The President is charged with the duty and invested with the power to take care that the laws be faithfully executed. The judiciary has jurisdiction to decide controversies between the States, and between their respective citizens, as well as questions of national concern; and the government is clothed with power to guarantee to every state a republican form of government, and to protect each of them against invasion and domestic violence. For the purpose of carrying into effect and executing these and the other powers conferred, and of providing for the common defence and general welfare, Congress is further invested with the taxing power in all its forms, except that of laying duties on exports, with the power to borrow money on the national credit, to punish crimes against the laws of the United States and of nations, to constitute courts, and to make all laws necessary and proper for carrying into execution the various powers vested in the government or any department or officer thereof.

Such being the character of the general government, it seems to be a self-evident proposition that it is invested with all those inherent and implied powers, which at the time of adopting the Constitution, were generally considered to belong to every government as such, and as being essential to the exercise of its functions. If this proposition be not true, it certainly is true that the government of the United States has express authority, in the clause last quoted, to make all such laws (usually regarded as inherent and implied) as may be necessary and proper for carrying on the government as constituted, and vindicating its authority and existence.

Another proposition equally clear is, that at the time the Constitution was adopted, it was, and had for a long time been, the practice of most, if not all, civilized governments, to employ the public credit as a means of anticipating the national revenues for the purpose of enabling them to exercise their governmental functions, and to meet the various exigencies to which all nations are subject; and that the mode of employing the public credit was various in different countries, and at different periods: sometimes by the agency of a national bank; sometimes by the issue of exchequer bills, or bills of credit; and sometimes by pledges of the public domain. In this country, the habit had prevailed from the commencement of the eighteenth century, of issuing bills of credit; and the revolution of independence had just been achieved, in great degree, by the means of similar bills issued by the Continental Congress. These bills were generally made a legal tender for the payment of all debts public and private, until, by the influence of English merchants at home, Parliament prohibited the issue of bills with that quality. This prohibition was first exercised in 1751, against the New England colonies; and subsequently, in 1763, against all the colonies. It was one of the causes of discontent which finally culminated in the revolution. Dr. FRANKLIN endeavored to obtain a repeal of the prohibitory acts, but only succeeded in obtaining from Parliament, in 1773, an act authorizing the colonies to make their bills receivable for taxes and debts due to the colony that issued them.

At the breaking out of the war, the Continental Congress commenced the issue of bills of credit, and the war was carried on without other resources for three or four years. It may be said with truth, that we owe our national independence to the use of this fiscal agency. Dr. FRANKLIN, in a letter to a friend, dated from Paris in April, 1779, after deploring the depreciation which the Continental Currency had undergone, said : " The only consolation under the evil is, that the public debt is proportionally diminished by the depreciation; and this by a kind of imperceptible tax, every one having paid a part of it in the fall of value that took place between the receiving and paying such sums as passed through his hands." He adds : " This effect of paper currency is not understood this side of the water. And, indeed, the whole is a mystery even to the politicians, how we have been able to continue a war four years without money, and how we could pay with paper, that had no previously fixed fund appropriated specially to redeem it. This currency, as we manage it, is a wonderful machine. It performs its office when we issue it; it pays and clothes troops, and provides victuals and ammunition."—(*Franklin's Works*, vol. 8, p. 329.) In a subsequent letter, of 9th October, 1780, he says : "They [the Congress] issued an immense quantity of paper bills, to pay, clothe, arm, and feed their troops, and fit out ships; and with this paper, without taxes for the first three years, they fought and battled one of the most powerful nations of Europe."—(*Works*, vol. 8, p. 507.) The Continental bills were not made legal-tenders at first, but in January, 1777, the Congress passed resolutions declaring that they ought to pass current in all payments, and be deemed in value equal to the same nominal sums in Spanish dollars; and that any one refusing so to receive them ought to be deemed an enemy to the liberties of the United States; and recommending to the legislatures of the several states to pass laws to that effect.—(*Journals of Cong.*, vol. 3, p. 19, 20 ; *Pitkin's Hist.*, vol. 2, p. 155.)

MASSACHUSETTS and other colonies, on the breaking out of the war, disregarded the prohibition of Parliament, and again conferred upon their bills the quality of legal tender.—(*Bancroft's Hist.*, vol. 7, 7 p. 324.)

These precedents are cited without reference to the policy or impolicy of the several measures in the particular cases; that is always a question for the legislative discretion. They establish the *historical fact* that when the Constitution was adopted, the employment of bills of credit was deemed a legitimate means of meeting the exigencies of a regularly constituted government, and that the affixing to them of the quality of a legal tender was regarded as entirely discretionary with the legislature. Such a quality was a mere incident that might or might not be annexed. The Continental Congress not being a regular government and not having the power to make laws for the regulation of private transactions, referred the matter to the state legislatures. The framers of the Constitution were familiar with all this history. They were familiar with the governments which had thus exercised the prerogative of issuing bills having the quality, and intended for the purposes referred to. They had first drawn their breath under these governments; they had helped to administer them. They had seen the important usages to which these securities might be applied.

In view, therefore, of all these facts, when we find them establishing the present government, with all the powers before rehearsed, giving to it, amongst other things, the sole control of the money of the country and expressly prohibiting the *states* from issuing bills of credit and from making any thing but gold and silver a legal tender, and imposing no such restriction upon the general government, how can we resist the conclusion that they intended to leave to it that power unimpaired, in case the future exigencies of the nation should require its exercise?

I am aware that according to the report of Mr. MADISON in the original draft of the Constitution, the clause relating to the borrowing of money, read, "to borrow money and emit bills on the credit of the United States," and that the words, "and emit bills," were, after some debate, struck out. But they were struck out with diverse views of members, some deeming them useless and others deeming them hurtful. The result was that they chose to adopt the Constitution as it now stands, without any words either of grant or restriction of power, and it is our duty to construe the instrument by its words, in the light of history, of the general nature of government, and the incidents of sovereignty.

The same argument was employed against the creation of a United States bank. A power to create corporations was proposed in the convention and rejected. The power was proposed with a limited application to cases where the public good might require them, and the authority of a single State might be incompetent. It was still rejected. It was then confined to the building of canals, but without effect. It was argued that such a power was unnecessary and might be dangerous. Yet Congress has not only chartered two United States banks, whose constitutionality has been sustained by this court, but several other institutions. As a means appropriate and conducive to the end of carrying into effect the other powers of the government, such as that of borrowing money with promptness and dispatch, and facilitating the fiscal operations of the government, it was deemed within the power of Congress to create such an institution under the general power given to pass all such laws as might be necessary and proper for carrying into execution the other powers granted. The views of particular members or the course of proceedings in the convention cannot control the fair meaning and general scope of the Constitution as it was finally framed and now stands. It is a finished document, complete in itself, and to be interpreted in the light of history and of the circumstances of the period in which it was framed.

No one doubts at the present day nor has ever seriously doubted that the power of the government to emit bills exists. It has been exercised by the government without question for a large portion of its history. This being conceded, the incidental power of giving such bills the quality of legal tender follows almost as a matter of course

I hold it to be the prerogative of every government, not restrained by its Constitution, to anticipate its resources by the issue of exchequer bills, bills of credit, bonds, stock, or a banking apparatus. Whether those issues shall or shall not be receivable in payment of private debts is an incidental matter in the discretion of such government unless restrained by constitutional prohibition.

This power is entirely distinct from that of coining money and regulating the value thereof. It is not only embraced in the power to make all necessary auxiliary laws, but it is incidental to the power of borrowing money. It is often a necessary means of anticipating and realizing promptly the national resources, when, perhaps, promptness is necessary to the national existence. It is not an attempt to coin money out of a valueless material, like the coinage of leather or ivory or kowrie shells. It is a pledge of the national credit. It is a promise by the government to pay dollars; it is not an attempt to make dollars. The standard of value is not changed. The government simply demands that its credit shall be accepted and received by public and private creditors during the pending exigency. Every government has a right to demand this when its existence is at stake. The interests of every citizen are bound up with the fate of the government. None can claim exemption. If they cannot trust their government in its time of trial they are not worthy to be its citizens.

But it is said, Why not borrow money in the ordinary way? The answer is, the legislative department, being the nation itself, speaking by its representatives, has a choice of methods, and is the master of its own discretion. One mode of borrowing, it is true, is to issue the government bonds and to invite capitalists to purchase them. But this is not the only mode. It is often too tardy and inefficient. In time of war or public danger, Congress, representing the sovereign power, by its right of eminent domain, may authorize the President to take private property for the public use and give government certificates therefor. This is largely done on such occasions. It is an indirect way of compelling the owner of property to lend to the government. He is forced to rely on the national debt.

Can the poor man's cattle and horses and corn be thus taken by the government when the public exigency requires it, and cannot the rich man's bonds and notes be in like manner taken to reach the same end? If the government enacts that the certificates of indebtedness which it gives to the farmer for his cattle and provender shall be receivable by the farmer's creditors in payment of his bonds and notes, is it anything more than transferring the government loan from the hands of one man to the hands of another—perhaps far more able to advance it? Is it anything more than putting the securities of the capitalist on the same platform as the farmer's stock?

No one supposes that these government certificates are never to be paid—that the day of specie payments is never to return. And it matters not in what form they are issued. The principle is still the same. Instead of certificates they may be treasury notes, or paper of any other form. And their payment may not be made directly in coin, but they may be first convertible into government bonds, or other government securities. Through whatever changes they pass, their ultimate destiny is *to be paid*. But it is the prerogative of the legislative department to determine when the fit time for payment has come. It may be long delayed, perhaps many may think it too long after the exigency has passed. But the abuse of a power, if proven, is no argument against its existence. And the courts are not responsible therefor. Questions of political expediency belong to the legislative halls, not to the judicial forum. It might subserve the present good if we should declare the legal-tender act unconstitutional, and a temporary public satisfaction might be the result. But what a miserable consideration would that be for a permanent loss of one of the just and necessary powers of the government: a power which, had Congress failed to exercise it when it did, we might have had no court here to-day to consider the question, nor a government or a country to make it important to do so.

Another ground of the power to issue treasury notes or bills is the necessity of providing a proper currency for the country, and especially of providing for the failure or disappearance of the ordinary currency in times of financial pressure and threatened collapse of commercial credit. Currency is a national necessity. The operations of the government, as well as private transactions, are wholly dependent upon it. The state governments are prohibited from making money or issuing bills. Uniformity of money was one of the objects of the Constitution. The coinage of money and regulation of its value is conferred upon the general government exclusively. That government has also the power to issue bills. It follows, as a matter of necessity, as a consequence of these various provisions, that it is specially the duty of the general government to provide a national currency. The states cannot do it, except by the charter of local banks, and that remedy, if strictly legitimate and constitutional, is inadequate, fluctuating, uncertain, and insecure, and operates with all the partiality to local interests, which it was the very object of the Constitution to avoid. But regarded as a duty of the general government, it is scarcely in accordance with the spirit of the Constitution, as well as in line with the national necessities.

It is absolutely essential to independent national existence that government should have a firm hold on the two great sovereign instrumentalities of the *sword* and the *purse*, and the right to wield them without restriction on occasions of national peril. In certain emergencies government must have at its command, not only the personal services—the bodies and lives—of its citizens, but the lesser, though not less essential, power of absolute control over the resources of the country. Its armies must be filled, and its navies manned, by the citizens in person. Its material of war, its munitions, equipment, and commissary stores must come from the industry of the country. This can only be stimulated into activity by a proper financial system, especially as regards the currency.

A constitutional government, notwithstanding the right of eminent domain, cannot take physical and forcible possession of all that it may need to defend the country, and is reluctant to exercise such a power when it can be avoided. *It must purchase*, and by purchase command materials and supplies, products of manufacture, labor, service of every kind. The government cannot, by physical power, compel the workshops to turn out millions of dollars' worth of manufactures in leather and cloth and wood and iron, which are the very first conditions of military equipment. It must stimulate and set in motion the industry of the country. In other words, it must *purchase*. But it cannot purchase with specie. That is soon exhausted, hidden or exported. It must purchase by *credit*. It cannot force its citizens to take its bonds. It must be able to lay its hands on the currency—that great instrument of exchange by which the people transact all their own affairs with each other; that thing which they must have, and which lies at the foundation of all industrial effort and all business in the community. When the ordinary currency disappears, as it often does in time of war; when business begins to stagnate and general bankruptcy is imminent, then the government must have power at the same time to renovate its own resources and to revive the drooping energies of the nation by supplying it with a circulating medium. What that medium shall be, what its character and qualities, will depend upon the greatness of the exigency, and the degree of promptitude which it demands. These are legislative questions. The heart of the nation must not be crushed out. The people must be aided to pay their debts and meet their obligations. The debtor interest of the country represents its bone and sinew, and must be encouraged to pursue its avocations. If relief were not afforded universal bankruptcy would ensue, and industry would be stopped, and government would be paralyzed in the paralysis of the people. It is an undoubted fact that during the late civil war, the activity of the workshops and factories, mines and machinery, ship-yards, railroads and canals of the loyal states, caused by the issue of the legal-tender currency, constituted an inexhaustible fountain of strength to the national cause.

These views are exhibited, not for the purpose of showing that the power is a desirable one, and therefore ought to be assumed; much less for the purpose of giving judgment on the expediency of its exercise in any particular case; but for the purpose of showing that it is one of those vital and essential powers inhering in every national sovereignty and necessary to its self-preservation.

But the creditor interest will lose some of its gold! Is gold the one thing needful? Is it worse for the creditor to lose a little by depreciation than everything by the bankruptcy of his debtor? Nay, is it worse than to lose everything by the subversion of the government? What is it that protects him in the accumulation and possession of his wealth? Is it not government and its laws? and can he not consent to trust that government for a brief period until it shall have vindicated its right to exist? All property and all rights, even those of liberty and life, are held subject to the fundamental condition of being liable to be impaired by providential calamities and national vicissitudes. Taxes impair my income or the value of my property. The condemnation of my homestead, or a valuable part of it for a public improvement, or public defence, will sometimes destroy its value to me; the conscription may deprive me of liberty and destroy my life. So with the power of government to borrow money, a power to be exercised by the consent of the lender, if possible, but to be exercised without his consent if necessary. And when exercised in the form of legal-tender notes or bills of credit, it may operate for the time being to compel the creditor to receive the *credit of the government* in place of the gold which he expected to receive from his debtor. All these are fundamental political conditions on which life, property and money are respectively held and enjoyed under our system of government—nay, under any system of government. There are times when the exigencies of the state rightly absorb all subordinate considerations of private interest, convenience, or feeling; and, at such times, the temporary, though compulsory, acceptance by a private creditor of the government credit, in lieu of his debtor's obligation to pay, is one of the slightest forms in which the necessary burdens of society can be sustained. Instead of being a violation of such obligation, it merely subjects it to one of those conditions under which it is held and enjoyed.

Another consideration bearing upon this objection is the fact that the power given to Congress to coin money and regulate the value thereof, includes the power to alter the metallic standard of coinage, as was done in 1834; whereby contracts made before the alteration and payable thereafter, were satisfied by the payment of six per cent. less of pure gold than was contemplated when the contracts were made. This power and this consequence flowing from its exercise were much discussed in the great case of MIXED MONEYS in Sir JOHN DAVIS' report, and it was there held to belong to the king's ordinary prerogative over the coinage of money, without any sanction from Parliament. Subsequent acts of Parliament fixed the standard of purity and weight in the coinage of the realm, which has not been altered for a hundred and fifty years past. But the same authority which fixed it in the time of Queen ANNE, is competent at any time to change it. Whether it shall be changed or not is a matter of mere legislative discretion. And such is undoubtedly the public law of this country. Therefore, the mere fact that the value of debts may be depreciated by legal-tender laws, is not conclusive against their validity; for that is clearly the effect of other powers which may be exercised by Congress in its discretion.

It follows as a corollary from these views, that it makes no difference in the principle of the thing, that the contract of the debtor is a specific engagement, in terms, to pay gold or silver money, or to pay in specie. So long as the money of the country, in whatever terms described, is in contemplation of the parties, it is the object of the legal-tender laws to make the credit of the government a lawful substitute therefor. If the contract is for the delivery of a chattel or a specific commodity or substance, the law does not apply. If it is bona fide for so many carats of diamonds or so many ounces of gold as bullion, the specific contract must be performed. But if terms which naturally import such a contract are used by way of evasion, and money only is intended, the law reaches the case. Not but that Congress might limit the operation of the law in any way it pleased. It might make an exception of cases where the contract expressly promises gold and silver money. But if it has not done so; if the enactment is general in its terms, specific promises to pay the money in specie are just as much subject to the operation of the law as a mere promise to pay so many dollars—for that, in contemplation of law, is a promise to pay money in specie.

Hence I differ from my brethren in the decision of one of the cases now before the court, to wit, the case of TREBILCOCK *vs.* WILSON, in which the promise (made in June, 1861) was to pay, one year after date, the sum of nine hundred dollars with ten per cent. interest from date, payable in specie. Of course this difference arises from the different construction given to the legal-tender acts. I do not understand the majority of the court to decide that an act so drawn as to embrace, in terms, contracts payable in specie, would not be constitutional. Such a decision would completely nullify the power claimed for the government. For it would be very easy, by the use of one or two additional words, to make all contracts payable in specie.

It follows as another corollary from the views which I have expressed that the power to make treasury notes a legal tender, whilst a mere incidental one to that of issuing the notes themselves, and to one of the forms of borrowing money, it is nevertheless a power not to be resorted to except upon extraordinary and pressing occasions, such as war or other public exigencies of great gravity and importance; and should be no longer exerted than all the circumstances of the case demand.

I do not say that it is a war power, or that it is only to be called into exercise in time of war; for other public exigencies may arise in the history of a nation which may make it expedient and imperative to exercise it. But of the occasions when, and of the times how long, it shall be exercised and in force, it is for the legislative department of the government to judge. Feeling sensibly the judgments and wishes of the people, that department cannot long (if it is proper to suppose that within its sphere it ever can) misunderstand the business interests and just rights of the community.

I deem it unnecessary to enter into a minute criticism of all the sayings, wise or foolish, that have, from time to time, been uttered on this subject by statesmen, philosophers, or theorists. The writers on political economy are generally opposed to the exercise of the power. The considerations which they adduce are very proper to be urged upon the depositary of the power. The question whether the power exists in a national government, is a great practical question relating to the national safety and independence, and statesmen are better judges of this question than economists can be. Their judgment is ascertained in the history and practice of governments, and in the silence as well as the words of our written Constitution. A parade of authorities would serve but little purpose after Chief Justice MARSHALL'S profound discussion of the powers of Congress in the great case of McCULLOH *vs*. THE STATE of MARYLAND. If we speak not according to the spirit of the Constitution and authorities, and the incontrovertible logic of events, elaborate extracts cannot add weight to our decision.

Great stress has been laid on the supposed fact that ENGLAND, in all its great wars and emergencies, has never made its exchequer bills a legal tender. This imports a eulogium on British conservatism in relation to contracts, which that nation would hardly regard as flattering. It is well known that for over twenty years, from 1797 to 1820, the most stringent paper money system that ever existed prevailed in ENGLAND and lay at the foundation of all her elasticity and endurance. It is true that the BANK OF ENGLAND notes, which the bank were required to issue until they reached an amount then unprecedented, were not technically made legal tenders, except for the purpose of relieving from arrest and imprisonment for debt; but worse than that, the bank was expressly *forbidden* to redeem its notes in specie, except for a certain small amount to answer the purpose of change. The people were obliged to receive them. The government had nothing else wherewith to pay its domestic creditors. The people themselves had no specie, for that was absorbed by the BANK OF ENGLAND, and husbanded for the uses of government in carrying on its foreign wars and paying its foreign subsidies. The country banks depended on the BANK OF ENGLAND for support, and of course they could not redeem their circulation in specie. The result was that the nation was perforce obliged to treat the bank notes as a legal tender or suffer inevitable bankruptcy. In such a state of things it went very hard with any man who demanded specie in fulfillment of his contracts. A man by the name of GRIGBY tried it, and brought his case into court, and elicited from Lord ALVANLY the energetic expression : "Thank God, few such creditors as the present plaintiff have been found since the passing of the act."—(2 *B. & P.*, 528.) It is to be presumed that he was the last that ever showed himself in an English court.

It is well known that since the resumption of specie payments, the act of 1833, rechartering the bank, has expressly made the BANK OF ENGLAND notes a legal tender.

It is unnecessary to refer to other examples. FRANCE is a notable one. Her assignats, issued at the commencement and during the revolution, performed the same office as our Continental bills; and enabled the nation to gather up its latent strength and call out its energies. Almost every nation of EUROPE, at one time or another, has found it necessary, or expedient, to resort to the same method of carrying on its operations or defending itself against aggression.

It would be sad, indeed, if this great nation were now to be deprived of a power so necessary to enable it to protect its own existence, and to cope with the other great powers of the world. No doubt, foreign powers would rejoice if we should deny the power. No doubt, foreign creditors would rejoice. They have, from the first, taken a deep interest in the question. But no true friend to our government, to its stability and its power to sustain itself under all vicissitudes, can be indifferent to the great wrong which it would sustain by a denial of the power in question—a power to be seldom exercised, certainly ; but one, the possession of which is so essential, and as it seems to me, so undoubted.

Regarding the question of power as so important to the stability of the government, I cannot acquiesce in the decision of HEPBURN vs. GRISWOLD (8 *Wallace*, 606). I cannot consent that the government should be deprived of one of its just powers by a decision made at the time, and under the circumstances, in which that decision was made. On a question relating to the power of the government, where I am perfectly satisfied that it has the power, I can never consent to abide by a decision denying it, unless made with responsible unanimity and acquiesced in by the country. Where the decision is recent, and is only made by a bare majority of the court, and during a time of public excitement on the subject, when the question has largely entered into the political discussions of the day, I consider it our right and duty to subject it to a further examination, if a majority of the court are dissatisfied with the former decision. And in this case, with all deference and respect for the former judgment of the court, I am so fully convinced that it was erroneous, and prejudicial to the rights, interests, and safety of the general government, that I, for one, have no hesitation in reviewing and overruling it. It should be remembered, that this court, at the very term in which, and within a few weeks after, the decision in HEPBURN vs. GRISWOLD was delivered, when the vacancies on the bench were filled, determined to hear the question re-argued. This fact must necessarily have had the effect of apprising the country that the decision was not fully acquiesced in, and of obviating any injurious consequences to the business of the country by its reversal.

In my judgment, the decrees in all the cases before us should be affirmed.

DISSENTING OPINION BY MR. CHIEF JUSTICE CHASE.

Before the Supreme Court of the United States,

December Term, 1870.

The cases of WILLIAM B. KNOX, *Plaintiff in Error, vs.* PHŒBE G. LEE *and* HUGH LEE, *her husband. In Error to the Circuit Court of the United States for the Western District of* TEXAS, *and*

THOMAS H. PARKER, *Plaintiff in Error, vs.* GEORGE DAVIS. *In error to the Supreme Judicial Court of the Commonwealth of* MASSACHUSETTS.

We dissent from the argument and conclusion in the opinion just announced.

The rule by which the constitutionality of an act of Congress passed in the alleged exercise of an implied power is to be tried, is no longer, in this court, open to question. It was laid down in the case of MCCULLOH *vs.* STATE OF MARYLAND, 4 *Wheaton*, 421, by Chief Justice MARSHALL, in these words: " Let the end be legitimate, let it be within the scope of this Constitution, and all means which are appropriate, which are plainly adapted to that end, which are not prohibited but consistent with the letter and spirit of the Constitution, are constitutional."

And it is the plain duty of the court to pronounce acts of Congress not made in the exercise of an express power nor coming within the reasonable scope of this rule, if made in virtue of an implied power, unwarranted by the Constitution. Acts of Congress not made in pursuance of the Constitution are not laws.

Neither of these propositions was questioned in the case of HEPBURN *vs.* GRISWOLD, 8 *Wallace*, 606. The judges who dissented in that case maintained that the clause in the act of February 25, 1862, making the United States notes a legal tender in payment of debts was an appropriate, plainly adapted means to a constitutional end, not prohibited but consistent with the letter and spirit of the Constitution. The majority of the court as then constituted, five judges out of eight, felt " obliged to conclude that an act making mere promises to pay dollars a legal tender in payments of debts previously contracted is not a means appropriate, plainly adapted, really calculated to carry into effect any express power vested in Congress, is inconsistent with the spirit of the Constitution, and is prohibited by the Constitution."

In the case of THE UNITED STATES *vs.* DE WITT, 9 *Wallace*, 41, we held unanimously that a provision of the internal revenue law prohibiting the sale of certain illuminating oil in the States was unconstitutional, though it might increase the production and sale of other oils, and consequently the revenue derived from them, because this consequence was too remote and uncertain to warrant the court in saying that the prohibition was an appropriate and plainly adapted means for carrying into execution the power to lay and collect taxes.

We agree, then, that the question whether a law is a necessary and proper means to execution of an express power, within the meaning of these words as defined by the rule, that is to say, a means appropriate, plainly adapted, not prohibited but consistent with the letter and spirit of the Constitution, is a judicial question. Congress may not adopt any means for the execution of an express power that Congress may see fit to adopt. It must be a necessary and proper means within the fair meaning of the rule. If not such it cannot be employed consistently with the Constitution. Whether the means actually employed in a given case are such or not, the court must decide. The court must judge of the fact—Congress of the degree of necessity.

A majority of the court, five to four, in the opinion which has just been read, reverses the judgment rendered by the former majority of five to three, in pursuance of an opinion formed after repeated arguments, at successive terms, and careful consideration; and declares the legal-tender clause to be constitutional; that is to say, that an act of Congress making promises to pay dollars legal tenders as coined dollars in payment of pre-existing debts is a means appropriate and plainly adapted to the exercise of powers expressly granted by the Constitution and not prohibited itself by the Constitution but consistent with its letter and spirit. And this reversal, unprecedented in the history of the court, has been produced by no change in the opinions of those who concurred in the former judgment. One closed an honorable judicial career by resignation after the case had been decided (27 November, 1869), after the opinion had been read and agreed to in conference (29 January, 1870), and after the day when it would have been delivered in court (31 January, 1870), had not the delivery been postponed for a week to give time for the preparation of the dissenting opinion. The court was then full, but the vacancy caused by the resignation of Mr. Justice GRIER having been subsequently filled and an additional justice having been appointed under the act increasing the number of judges to nine, which took effect on the first Monday of December, 1869, the then majority find themselves in a minority of the court, as now constituted, upon the question.

Their convictions, however, remain unchanged. We adhere to the opinion pronounced in HEPBURN vs. GRISWOLD. Reflection has only wrought a firmer belief in the soundness of the constitutional doctrines maintained, and in the importance of them to the country.

We agree that much of what was said in the dissenting opinion in that case, which has become the opinion of the majority of the court as now constituted, was correctly said. We fully agree in all that was quoted from Chief Justice MARSHALL. We had indeed accepted, without reserve, the definition of implied powers in which that great judge summed up his argument, of which the language quoted formed a part. But if it was intended to ascribe to us "the doctrine that when an act of Congress is brought to the test of this clause of the Constitution," namely, the clause of granting the power of ancillary legislation, "its necessity must be absolute, and its adaptation to the conceded purpose unquestionable," we must be permitted not only to disclaim it, but to say that there is nothing in the opinion of the then majority which approaches the assertion of any such doctrine.

We did indeed venture to cite, with approval, the language of Judge STORY in his great work on the Constitution, that the words "necessary and proper" were intended to have "a sense at once admonitory and directory," and to require that the means used in the execution of an express power "should be *bona fide*, appropriate to the end (1 *Story on the Constitution*, p. 42, sec. 1,251), and also ventured to say that the tenth amendment, reserving to the states or the people all powers not delegated to the United States by the Constitution, nor prohibited by it to the states, "was intended to have a like admonitory and directory sense," and to restrain the limited government established by the Constitution from the exercise of powers not clearly delegated or derived by just inference from powers so delegated. In thus quoting Judge STORY, and in this expression of our own opinion, we certainly did not suppose it possible that we could be understood as asserting that the clause in question "was designed as a restriction upon the ancillary power incidental to every grant of power in express terms." It was this proposition which "was stated and refuted" in MCCULLOH *vs.* STATE OF MARYLAND. That refutation touches nothing said by us. We assert only that the words of the Constitution are such as admonish Congress that implied powers are not to be rashly or lightly assumed, and that they are not to be exercised at all, unless, in the words of Judge STORY, they are "*bona fide*, appropriate to the end," or, in the words of Chief Justice MARSHALL, "appropriate, plainly adapted" to a constitutional and legitimate end, and "not prohibited, but consistent with the letter and spirit of the Constitution."

There appears, therefore, to have been no real difference of opinion in the court as to the rule by which the existence of an implied power is to be tested, when HEPBURN *vs.* GRISWOLD, 8 *Wallace*, 606, was decided, though the then minority seem to have supposed there was. The difference had reference to the application of the rule rather than to the rule itself.

The then minority admitted that in the powers relating to coinage, standing alone, there is not "a sufficient warrant for the exercise of the power" to make notes a legal tender, but thought them "not without decided weight, when we come to consider the question of the existence of this power as one necessary and proper for carrying into execution other admitted powers of the government." This weight they found in the fact that an "express power over the lawful money of the country was confided to Congress and forbidden to the states." It seemed to them not an "unreasonable inference" that, in a certain contingency, "making the securities of the government perform the office of money in the payment of debts would be in harmony with the power expressly granted to coin money." We percieve no connection between the express power to coin money and the inference that the government may in any contingency, make its securities perform the functions of coined money, as a legal tender in payment of debts. We have supposed that the power to exclude from circulation notes not authorized by the national government might, perhaps, be deduced from the power to regulate the value of coin; but that the power of the government to emit bills of credit was an exercise of the power to borrow money, and that its power over the currency was incidental to that power and to the power to regulate commerce. This was the doctrine of the VEAZIE BANK *vs.* FENNO, 8 *Wallace*, 533–548, although not fully elaborated in that case. The question whether the quality of legal tender can be imparted to these bills depends upon distinct considerations.

Was, then, the power to make these notes of the government—these bills of credit—a legal tender in payments an appropriate, plainly-adapted means to a legitimate and constitutional end? or, to state the question as the opinion of the then minority stated it, "does there exist any power in Congress, or in the government, by express grant, in execution of which this legal-tender act was necessary and proper in the sense here defined and under the circumstances of its passage?"

The opinion of the then minority affirmed the power on the ground that it was a necessary and proper means, within the definition of the court, in the case of McCULLOH *vs.* MARYLAND, to carry on war, and that it was not prohibited by the spirit or letter of the Constitution, though it was admitted to be a law impairing the obligation of contracts, and notwithstanding the objection that it deprived many persons of their property without compensation and without due process of law.

We shall not add much to what was said in the opinion of the then majority on these points.

The reference made in the opinion just read, as well as in the argument at the bar, to the opinions of the Chief Justice, when Secretary of the Treasury, seems to warrant, if it does not require, some observations before proceeding further in the discussion.

It was his fortune at the time the legal-tender clause was inserted in the bill to authorize the issue of United States notes, and received the sanction of Congress, to be charged with the anxious and responsible duty of providing funds for the prosecution of the war.

In no report made by him to Congress was the expedient of making the notes of the United States a legal tender suggested. He urged the issue of notes payable on demand in coin or received as coin in payment of duties. When the State banks had suspended specie payments, he recommended the issue of United States notes receivable for all loans to the United States and all government dues except duties on imports. In his report of December, 1862, he said that "United States notes receivable for bonds bearing a secure specie interest are next best to notes convertible into coin," and after stating the financial measures which in his judgment were advisable, he added: "The Secretary recommends, therefore, no mere paper money scheme, but on the contrary a series of measures looking to a safe and gradual return to gold and silver as the only permanent basis, standard, and measure of value recognized by the Constitution."

At the session of Congress before this report was made, the bill containing the legal-tender clause had become a law. He was extremely and avowedly averse to this clause, but was very solicitous for the passage of the bill to authorize the issue of United States notes then pending. He thought it indispensably necessary that the authority to issue these notes should be granted by Congress. The passage of the bill was delayed, if not jeoparded, by the difference of opinion which prevailed on the question of making them a legal tender. It was under these circumstances that he expressed the opinion, when called upon by the Committee of Ways and Means, that it was necessary;* and he was not sorry to find it sustained by the decision of respected courts, not unanimous indeed, nor without contrary decisions of state courts equally respectable.

Examination and reflection under more propitious circumstances have satisfied him that this opinion was erroneous, and he does not hesitate to declare it. He would do so, just as unhesitatingly, if his favor to the legal-tender clause had been at that time decided, and his opinion as to the constitutionality of the measure clear.

Was the making of the notes a legal tender necessary to the carrying on the war? In other words, was it necessary to the execution of the power to borrow money? It is not the question whether the issue of notes was necessary, nor whether any of the financial measures of the government were necessary. The issuing of the circulation commonly known as greenbacks, was necessary and constitutional. They were necessary to the payment of the army and the navy and to all the purposes for which the government uses money. The banks had suspended specie payment, and the government was reduced to the alternative of using their paper or issuing its own.

Now, it is a common error, and in our judgment it was the error of the opinion of the minority in HEPBURN *vs.* GRISWOLD, 8 *Wallace*, 606, and is the error of the opinion just read, that considerations pertinent to the issue of United States notes have been urged in justification of making them a legal tender. The real question is, was the making them a legal tender a necessary means to the execution of the power to borrow money? If the notes would circulate as well without as with this quality, it is idle to urge the plea of such necessity.

But the circulation of the notes was amply provided for by making them receivable for all national taxes, all dues to the government, and all loans. This was the provision relied upon for the purpose by

---

* Letters of the Secretary of the Treasury to the Committee of Ways and Means, January 22 and 29, 1862; *Spaulding's Financial History, pp.* 27, 46, 54.

the secretary when the bill was first prepared, and his impression then and his reflections since have convinced him that it was sufficient. Nobody could pay a tax, or any debt, or buy a bond without using these notes. As the notes, not being immediately redeemable, would undoubtedly be cheaper than coin, they would be preferred by debtors and purchasers. They would thus, by the universal law of trade, pass into general circulation. As long as they were maintained by the government at or near par value of specie, they would be accepted in payment of all dues private as well as public. Debtors, as a general rule, would pay in nothing else unless compelled by suit, and creditors would accept them as long as they would lose less by acceptance than by suit.

In new transactions sellers would demand and purchasers would pay the premium for specie in the prices of commodities. The difference to them in the currency, whether of coin or of paper, would be in the fluctuations to which the latter is subject.

So long as notes should not sink so low as to induce creditors to refuse to receive them because they could not be said to be in any just sense payments of debts due, a provision for making them a legal tender would be without effect except to discredit the currency to which it was applied.

The real support of note circulation not convertible on demand into coin, is receivability for debts due the government, including specie loans, and limitation of amount.

If the amount is smaller than is needed for the transactions of the country, and the law allows the use in these transactions of but one description of currency, the demand for that description will prevent its depreciation. But history shows no instance of paper issues so restricted. An approximation in limitation is all that is possible, and this was attempted when the issues of United States notes were restricted to one hundred and fifty millions. But this limit was soon extended to four hundred and fifty millions, and even this was soon practically removed by the provision for the issue of notes by the national banking associations without any provision for corresponding reduction in the circulation of United States notes; and still further by the laws authorizing the issue of interest-bearing securities, made a tender for their amount, excluding interest.

The best support for note circulation is not limitation but receivability, especially for loans bearing coin interest. This support was given until the fall of 1864, when a loan bearing increased currency interest, payable in three years and convertible into a loan bearing less coin interest, was substituted for the six per cent. and five per cent. loans bearing specie interest, for which the notes had been previously received.

It is plain that a currency so supported cannot depreciate more than the loans; in other words, below the general credit of the country. It will rise or fall with it. At the present moment, if the notes were received for five per cent. bonds, they would be at par. In other words, specie payments would be resumed.

Now, does making the notes a legal tender increase their value? It is said that it does, by giving them a new use. The best political economists say that it does not.

When the government compels the people to receive its notes, it virtually declares that it does not expect them to be received without compulsion. It practically represents itself insolvent. This certainly does not improve the value of its notes. It is an element of depreciation.

In addition, it creates a powerful interest in the debtor class and in the purchasers of bonds to depress to the lowest point the credit of the notes. The cheaper these become, the easier the payment of debts and the more profitable the investments in bonds bearing coin interest.

On the other hand, the higher prices become, for everything the government needs to buy, and the greater the accumulation of public as well as private debt.

It is true that such a state of things is acceptable to debtors, investors in bonds, and speculators. It is their opportunity of relief or wealth. And many are persuaded by their representations that the forced circulation is not only a necessity, but a benefit. But the apparent benefit is a delusion, and the necessity imaginary.

In their legitimate use, the notes are hurt, not helped, by being made a legal tender. The legal-tender quality is only valuable for the purposes of dishonesty. Every honest purpose is answered as well and better without it.

We have no hesitation, therefore, in declaring our conviction that the making of these notes a legal tender, was not a necessary or proper means to the carrying on war or to the exercise of any express power of the government.

But the absence of necessity is not our only, or our weightiest, objection to this legal-tender clause. We still think, notwithstanding the argument adduced to the contrary, that it does violate an express provision of the Constitution, and the spirit, if not the letter, of the whole instrument.

It cannot be maintained that legislation justly obnoxious to such objections can be maintained as the exercise of an implied power. There can be no implication against the Constitution. Legislation, to be warranted as the exercise of implied powers, must not be "prohibited, but consistent with the letter and spirit of the Constitution."

The fifth amendment provides that no person shall be deprived of life, liberty, or property, without compensation or due process of law. The opinion of the former minority says that the argument against the validity of the legal-tender clause, founded on this constitutional provision, is "too vague for their perception." It says that a "declaration of war would be thus unconstitutional," because it might depreciate the value of property; and "the abolition of tariff on sugar, or iron," because it might destroy the capital employed in those manufactures; and "the successive issues of government, bonds," because they might make those already in private hands less valuable. But it seems to have escaped the attention of the then minority that to declare war, to lay and repeal taxes, and to borrow money, are all express powers, and that the then majority were opposing the prohibition of the Constitution to the claim of an implied power. Besides, what resemblance is there between the effect of the exercise of these express powers and the operation of the legal-tender clause upon pre-existing debts? The former are indirect effects of the exercise of undisputed powers. The latter acts directly upon the relations of debtor and creditor. It violates that fundamental principle of all just legislation that the legislature shall not take the property of A and give it to B. It says that B, who has purchased a farm of A for a certain price, may keep the farm without paying for it, if he will only tender certain notes which may bear some proportion to the price, or be even worthless. It seems to us that this is a manifest violation of this clause of the Constitution.

We think, also, that it is inconsistent with the spirit of the Constitution in that it impairs the obligation of contracts. In the opinion of the then minority, it is frankly said: "Undoubtedly it is a law impairing the obligation of contracts made before its passage," but it is immediately added: "While the Constitution forbids the states to pass such laws, it does not forbid Congress," and this opinion, as well as the opinion just read, refers to the express authority to establish a uniform system of bankruptcy as a proof that it was not the intention of the Constitution to withhold that power. It is true that the Constitution grants authority to pass a bankrupt law, but our inference is, that in this way only can Congress discharge the obligation of contracts. It may provide for ascertaining the inability of debtors to perform their contracts, and, upon the surrender of all their property, may provide for their discharge. But this is a very different thing from providing that they may satisfy contracts without payment, without pretence of inability, and without any judicial proceeding.

That Congress possesses the general power to impair the obligation of contracts is a proposition which, to use the language of Chief Justice MARSHALL (FLETCHER vs. PECK, 6 Cr., 132), "must find its vindication in a train of reasoning not often heard in courts of justice." "It may well be added," said the great judge (IBID., 135), "whether the nature of society and of government does not prescribe some limits to legislative power; and, if any be prescribed, where are they to be found, if the property of an individual, fairly and honestly acquired, can be seized without compensation? To the legislature all legislative power is granted, but the question whether the act of transferring the property of an individual to the public is in the nature of a legislative power is well worthy of serious reflection."

And if the property of an individual cannot be transferred to the public, how much less to another individual?

These remarks of Chief Justice MARSHALL were made in a case in which it became necessary to determine whether a certain act of the legislature of Georgia was within the constitutional prohibition against impairing the obligation of contracts. And they assert fundamental principles of society and government in which that prohibition had its origin. They apply with great force to the construction of the Constitution of the United States. In like manner and spirit Mr. Justice CHASE had previously declared (CALDER vs. BULL, 3 *Dallas*, 388) than "an act of the legislature contrary to the great first principles of the social compact cannot be considered a rightful exercise of legislative authority." Among such acts he instances "a law that destroys or impairs the lawful exercise of legislative authority." Among such acts he instances "a law that destroys or impairs the lawful private contracts of citizens." Can we be mistaken in saying that such a law is contrary to the spirit of a Constitution ordained to establish justice ? Can we be mistaken in thinking that if MARSHALL and STORY were here to pronounce judgment in this case they would declare the legal-tender clause now in question to be prohibited by and inconsistent with the letter and spirit of the Constitution ?

It is unnecessary to say that we reject wholly the doctrine, advanced for the first time, we believe, in this court, by the present majority, that the legislature has any "powers under the Constitution which grow out of the aggregate of powers conferred upon the government, or out of the sovereignty instituted by it." If this proposition be admitted, and it be also admitted that the legislature is the sole judge of the necessity for the exercise of such powers, the government becomes practically absolute and unlimited.

Our observations thus far have been directed to the question of the constitutionality of the legal-tender clause and its operation upon contracts made before the passage of the law. We shall now consider whether it be constitutional in its application to contracts made after its passage. In other words, whether Congress has power to make anything but coin a legal tender.

And here it is well enough again to say that we do not question the authority to issue notes or to fit them for a circulating medium or to promote their circulation by providing for their receipt in payment of debts to the government, and for redemption either in coin or in bonds; in short, to adapt them to use as currency. Nor do we question the lawfulness of contracts stipulating for payment in such notes or the propriety of enforcing the performance of such contracts by holding the tender of such currency, according to their terms, sufficient. The question is, has Congress power to make the notes of the government, redeemable or irredeemable, a legal tender without contract and against the will of the person to whom they are tendered ? In considering this question, we assume as a fundamental proposition that it is the duty of every government to establish a standard of value.

The necessity of such a standard is indeed universally acknowledged. Without it the transactions of society would become impossible.

All measures, whether of extent or weight or value, must have certain proportions of that which they are intended to measure. The unit of extent must have certain definite length, the unit of weight certain definite gravity, and the unit of value certain definite value. These units, multiplied or subdivided, supply the standards by which all measures are properly made.

The selection, therefore, by the common consent of all nations, of gold and silver as the standard of value was natural, or, more correctly speaking, inevitable. For whatever definitions of value political economists may have given, they all agree that gold and silver have more value in proportion to weight and size, and are less subject to loss by wear or abrasion than any other material capable of easy subdivision and impression, and that their value changes less and by slower degrees, through considerable periods of time, than that of any other substance which could be used for the same purpose. And these are qualities indispensable to the convenient use of the standard required.

In the construction of the constitutional grant of power to establish a standard of value, *every presumption* is, therefore, against that which would authorize the adoption of any other materials than those sanctioned by universal consent.

But the terms of the only express grant in the Constitution of power to establish such a standard leave little room for presumptions. The power conferred is the power to coin money, and these words must be understood as they were used at the time the Constitution was adopted. And we have been referred to no authority which at that time defined coining otherwise than as minting or stamping metals for money; or money otherwise than as metal coined for the purposes of commerce. These are the words of JOHNSON, whose great dictionary contains no reference to money of paper.

It is true that notes issued by banks, both in ENGLAND and AMERICA, were then in circulation, and were used in exchanges and in common speech called money, and that bills of credit, issued both by Congress and by the states, had been recently in circulation under the same general name; but these notes and bills were never regarded as real money, but were always treated as its representatives only, and were described as currency. The legal-tender notes themselves do not purport to be anything else than promises to pay money. They have been held to be securities, and therefore exempt from state taxation; (BANK *vs.* SUPERVISORS, 7 *Wallace*, 31,) and the idea that it was ever designed to make such notes a standard of value by the framers of the Constitution is wholly new. It seems to us impossible that it could have been entertained. Its assertion seems to us to ascribe folly to the framers of our fundamental law, and to contradict the most conspicuous facts in our public history.

The power to coin money was a power to determine the fineness, weight, and denominations of the metallic pieces by which values were to be measured; and we do not perceive how this meaning can be extended without doing violence to the very words of the Constitution by imposing on them a sense they were never intended to bear.

This construction is supported by contemporaneous and all subsequent action of the legislature; by all the recorded utterances of statesmen and jurists, and the unbroken tenor of judicial opinion until a very recent period, when the excitement of the civil war led to the adoption, by many, of different views.

The sense of the convention which framed the Constitution is clear, from the account given by Mr. MADISON of what took place when the power to emit bills of credit was stricken from the reported draft. He says distinctly that he acquiesced in the motion to strike out, because the government would not be disabled thereby from the use of public notes, so far as they would be safe and proper, while it cut off the pretext for a paper currency, and particularly for making the bills a tender either for public or private debts.—(3 *Madison Papers*, 1,346.) The whole discussion upon bills of credit proves, beyond all possible questions, that the convention regarded the power to make notes a legal tender as absolutely excluded from the Constitution.

The papers of the *Federalist*, widely circulated in favor of the ratification of the Constitution, discuss briefly the power to coin money, as a power to fabricate metallic money, without a hint that any power to fabricate money of any other description was given to Congress (*Dawson's Federalist*, 294); and the views which it promulgated may be fairly regarded as the views of those who voted for adoption.

Acting upon the same views, Congress took measures for the establishment of a mint, exercising thereby the power to coin money, and has continued to exercise the same power, in the same way, until the present day. It established the dollar as the money unit, determined the quantity and quality of gold and silver of which each coin should consist, and prescribed the denominations and forms of all coins to be issued.—(1 *U. S. St.*, 225, 246, *and subsequent acts.*) Until recently no one in Congress ever suggested that that body possessed power to make anything else a standard of value.

Statesmen who have disagreed widely on other points have agreed in the opinion that the only constitutional measures of value are metallic coins, struck as regulated by the authority of Congress. Mr. WEBSTER expressed not only his opinion, but the universal and settled conviction of the country when he said: (4 *Webster's Works*, 271, 280) " Most unquestionably there is no legal tender, and there can be no legal tender in this country, under the authority of this government or any other, but gold and silver, either the coinage of our mints or foreign coins at rates regulated by Congress. This is a constitutional principle perfectly plain and of the very highest importance. The states are prohibited from making anything but gold and silver a tender in payment of debts, and although no such express prohibition is applied to Congress, *yet as Congress has no power granted to it in this respect but to coin money and regulate the value of foreign coin*, it clearly has no power to substitute paper or anything else for coin as a tender in payment of debts and in discharge of contracts."

And this court, in GWIN *vs.* BREEDLOVE (2 *Howard*, 38), said : " *By the Constitution of the United States gold and silver coin* made current by law *can only be tendered* in payment of debts." And in THE UNITED STATES *vs.* MARIGOLD (9 *Howard,* 567), this court, speaking of the trust and duty of maintaining a uniform and pure metallic standard of uniform value throughout the Union, said : " The power of coining money and regulating its value *was delegated to Congress by the Constitution for the very purpose,* as assigned by the framers of that instrument, *of creating and preserving the uniformity and purity of such a standard of value."*

The present majority of the court say that legal-tender notes " have become the universal measure of values," and they hold that the legislation of Congress, substituting such measures for coin by making the notes a legal tender in payment, is warranted by the Constitution.

But if the plain sense of words, if the contemporaneous exposition of parties, if common consent in understanding, if the opinions of courts, avail anything in determining the meaning of the Constitution, it seems impossible to doubt that the power to coin money is a power to establish a uniform standard of value, and that no other power to establish such a standard, by making notes a legal tender, is conferred upon Congress by the Constitution.

My brothers CLIFFORD and FIELD concur in these views, but in consideration of the importance of the principles involved will deliver their separate opinions. My brother NELSON also dissents.

DISSENTING OPINION BY MR. JUSTICE CLIFFORD.

Before the Supreme Court of the United States,
December Term, 1870.

The cases of WILLIAM B. KNOX, *Plaintiff in Error, vs.* PHŒBE G. LEE *and* HUGH LEE, *her husband. In Error to the Circuit Court of the United States for the Western District of* TEXAS,
and
THOMAS H. PARKER, *Plaintiff in Error, vs.* GEORGE DAVIS. *In error to the Supreme Judicial Court of the Commonwealth of* MASSACHUSETTS.

Money, in the constitutional sense, means coins of gold and silver fabricated and stamped by authority of law as a measure of value, pursuant to the power vested in Congress by the Constitution.—(WALKER'S *Science of Wealth,* 124. LIVERPOOL *on Coins,* 8.)

Coins of copper may also be minted for small fractional circulation, as authorized by law and the usage of the government for eighty years, but it is not necessary to discuss that topic at large in this investigation.—(JEFFERSON'S *Works,* 462.)

Even the authority of Congress upon the general subject does not extend beyond the power to coin money, regulate the value thereof and of foreign coin.—(*Const.,* art. 8, clause 5.)

Express power is also conferred upon Congress to fix the standard of weights and measures, and of course that standard, as applied to future transactions, may be varied or changed to promote the public interest, but the grant of power in respect to the standard of value is expressed in more guarded language, and the grant is much more restricted.

Power to fix the standard of weights and measures is evidently a power of comparatively wide discretion, but the power to regulate the value of the money authorized by the Constitution to be coined is a definite and precise grant of power, admitting of very little discretion in its exercise, and is not equivalent, except to a very limited extent, to the power to fix the standard of weights and measures, as the money authorized by that clause of the Constitution is coined money, and as a necessary consequence must be money of actual value, fabricated from the precious metals generally used for that purpose at the period when the Constitution was framed.

Coined money, such as is authorized by that clause of the instrument, consists only of the coins of the United States fabricated and stamped by authority of law, and is the same money as that described in the next clause of the same section as the current coins of the United States, and is the same money also as "the gold and silver coins" described in the tenth section of the same article, which prohibits the states from coining money, emitting bills of credit, or making " anything but gold and silver coin a tender in payment of debts."

Intrinsic value exists in gold and silver, as well before as after it is fabricated and stamped as coin, which shows conclusively that the principal discretion vested in Congress under that clause of the Constitution consists in the power to determine the denomination, fineness, or value and description of the coins to be struck, and the relative proportion of gold or silver, whether standard or pure, and the proportion of alloy to be used in minting the coins, and to prescribe the mode in which the intended object of the grant shall be accomplished and carried into practical effect.

Discretion, to some extent, in prescribing the value of the coins minted, is beyond doubt vested in Congress, but the plain intent of the Constitution is that Congress, in determining that matter, shall be governed chiefly by the weight and intrinsic value of the coins, as it is clear that if the stamped value of the same should much exceed the real value of gold and silver not coined, the minted coins would immediately cease to be either current coins or a standard of value as contemplated by the Constitution.—(HUSKISSON *on Depreciation of Currency*, 22 *Financial Pamphlets*, 579.)

Commercial transactions imperiously require a standard of value, and the commercial world, at a very early period in civilization, adopted gold and silver as the true standard for that purpose, and the standard originally adopted has ever since continued to be so regarded by universal consent to the present time.

Paper currency has, at one time or another, been authorized and employed as such by most commercial nations, and by no government, past or present, more extensively than by the United States, and yet it is safe to affirm that all experience in its use as a circulating medium has demonstrated the proposition that it cannot by any legislation, however stringent, be made a standard of value or the just equivalent of gold and silver. Attempts of the kind have always failed, and no body of men, whether in public or private stations, ever had more instructive teachings of the truth of that remark than the patriotic men who framed the Federal Constitution, as they had seen the power to emit bills of credit freely exercised during the war of the revolution, not only by the Confederation but also by the states, and knew from bitter experience its calamitous effects and the utter worthlessness of such a circulating medium as a standard of value. Such men so instructed could not have done otherwise than they did do, which was to provide an irrepealable standard of value, to be coined from gold and silver, leaving as little upon the subject to the discretion of Congress as was consistent with a wise forecast and an invincible determination that the essential principles of the Constitution should be perpetual as the means to secure the blessings of liberty to themselves and their posterity.

Associated as the grant to coin money and regulate the value thereof is with the grant to fix the standard of weights and measures, the conclusion, when that fact is properly weighed in connection with the words of the grant, is irresistible that the purpose of the framers of the Constitution was to provide a permanent standard of value, which should, at all times and under all circumstances, consist of coin, fabricated and stamped, from gold and silver, by anthority of law, and that they intended at the same time to withhold from Congress, as well as from the states, the power to substitute any other money as a standard of value in matters of finance, business, trade, or commerce.

Support to that view may also be drawn from the last words of the clause giving Congress the unrestricted power to regulate the value of foreign coin, as it would be difficult if not impossible to give full effect to the standard of value prescribed by the Constitution, in times of fluctuation, if the circulating medium could be supplied by foreign coins not subject to any congressional regulation as to their value.

Exclusive power to regulate the alloy and value of the coin struck by their own authority, or by the authority of the states, was vested in Congress under the Confederation, but the Congress was prohibited from enacting any regulation as to the value of the coins unless nine states assented to the proposed regulation.

Subject to the power of Congress to pass such regulations it is unquestionably true that the states, under the Confederation as well as the United States, possessed the power to coin money, but the Constitution, when it was adopted, denied to the states all authority upon the subject, and also ordained that they should not make any thing but gold and silver coin a tender in payment of debts.

Beyond all doubt the framers of the Constitution intended that the money unit of the United States, for measuring values, should be one dollar, as the word dollar in the plural form is employed in the body of the Constitution, and also in the seventh amendment, recommended by Congress at its first session after the Constitution was adopted. Two years before that, to wit, July 6, 1785, the Congress of the Confederation enacted that the money unit of the United States should "be one dollar," and one year later, to wit, August 8, 1786, they established the standard for gold and silver, and also provided that the money of account of the United States should correspond with the coins established by law.—(1 *Laws U. S.*, 1st ed., 646. 1 *Curtis' Hist. Const.*, 443. X. *Journ. Cong.* (*Dunlaps' ed.*), 225. 1 *Life Gouverneur Morris*, 273. XI. *Journ. Cong.*, 179.)

On the fourth of March, 1789, Congress first assembled under the Constitution, and proceeded without unnecessary delay to enact such laws as were necessary to put the government in operation, which the Constitution had ordained and established. Ordinances had been passed during the Confederation to organize the executive departments, and for the establishment of a mint, but the new Constitution did not perpetuate any of those laws, and yet Congress continued to legislate for a period of three years before any new law was passed prescribing the money unit or the money of account, either for "the public offices" or for the courts. Throughout that period it must have been understood that those matters were impliedly regulated by the Constitution, as tariffs were enacted, tonnage duties imposed, laws passed for the collection of duties, the several executive departments created, and the judiciary of the United States organized and empowered to exercise full jurisdiction under the Constitution.

Duties of tonnage and import duties were required, by the act of the thirty-first of July, 1789, to be paid "in gold and silver coin," and Congress in the same act adopted comprehensive regulations as to the value of foreign coin, but no provision was made for coining money or for a standard of value, except so far as that subject is involved in the regulation as to the value of foreign coin, or for a money unit, nor was any regulation prescribed as to the money of account. Revenue for the support of the government, under those regulations, was to be derived solely from duties of tonnage and import duties, and the express provision was that those duties should be collected in gold and silver coin.—(1 *Statutes at Large*, 24. 1 *Ibid.*, 29.)

Legislation under the Constitution had proceeded thus far before the Treasury Department was created. Treasury regulations for the collection, safe-keeping, and disbursement of the public moneys became indispensable, and Congress, on the second of September, 1789, passed the act to establish the Treasury Department, which has ever since remained in force.—(1 *Statutes at Large*, 65.)

By that act the Secretary of the Treasury is declared to be the head of the department, and it is made his duty, among other things, to digest and prepare plans for the improvement and management of the public finances and for the support of the public credit; to prepare and report estimates of the public revenue and of the public expenditures; to superintend the collection of the revenue; to prescribe forms of keeping and stating accounts and for making returns; to grant all warrants for moneys to be issued from the treasury, in pursuance of appropriations by law, and to perform all such services relative to the finances as he shall be directed to perform.

Moneys collected from duties of tonnage and from import duties constituted at that period the entire resources of the national treasury, and the antecedent act of Congress, providing for the collection of those duties, imperatively required that all such duties should be paid in gold and silver coin, from which it follows that the moneys mentioned in the act creating the Treasury Department were moneys of gold and silver coin which were collected as public revenue from the duties of tonnage and import duties imposed by the before-mentioned prior acts of Congress. Appropriations made by Congress were understood as appropriations of moneys in the treasury, and all warrants issued by the Secretary of the Treasury were understood to be warrants for the payment of gold and silver coin. Forms for keeping and stating accounts, and for making returns and for warrants for moneys to be issued from the treasury were prescribed, and in all those forms the Secretary of the Treasury adopted the money unit recognized in the Constitution and which had been ordained four years before by the Congress of the Confederation.

Argument to show that the national treasury was organized on the basis that the gold and silver coins of the United States were to be the standard of value is unnecessary, as it is a historical fact which no man or body of men can ever successfully contradict. Public attention had been directed to the necessity of establishing a mint for the coinage of gold and silver, several years before the convention met to frame the Constitution, and a committee was appointed by the Congress of the Confederation to consider and report upon the subject. They reported on the twenty-first of February, 1782, more than a year before the treaty of peace, in favor of creating such an establishment, and on the sixteenth of October, 1786, the Congress adopted an ordinance providing that a mint should be established for the coinage of gold, silver, and copper, agreeably to the resolves of Congress previously mentioned, which prescribed the standard of gold and silver, and recognized the money unit established by the resolves passed in the preceding year.—(1 *Laws U. S.*, 647. X. *Journals Congress*, 225. XI. *Journals Congress*, 254. 8 *Statutes at Large*, 80.)

Congressional legislation organizing the new government had now progressed to the point where it became necessary to re-examine that subject and to make provision for the exercise of the power to coin money, as authorized by the Constitution. Pursuant to that power Congress, on the second of April, 1792, passed the act establishing a mint for the purpose of a national coinage, and made provision, among other things, that coins of gold and silver, of certain fineness and weight, and of certain denominations, value, and descriptions, should be from time to time struck and coined at the said mint. Specific provision is there made for coining gold and silver coins, as follows : First, gold coins, to wit : Eagles of the value of ten dollars or units ; half-eagles of the value of five dollars ; quarter-eagles of the value of two-and-a-half dollars, the act specifying in each case the number of grains and fractions of a grain the coin shall contain, whether fabricated from pure or standard gold. Second, silver coins, to wit : " DOLLARS OR UNITS," each to contain three hundred and seventy-one grains and four-sixteenth parts of a grain of pure silver, or four hundred and sixteen grains of standard silver. Like provision is also made for the coinage of half-dollars, quarter-dollars, dimes and half-dimes, and also for the coinage of certain copper coins, but it is not necessary to enter much into those details in this case.

Provision, it must be conceded, is not there made, in express terms, that the money unit of the United States shall be one dollar, as in the ordinance passed during the Confederation, but the act under consideration assumes throughout that the coin called dollar is the coin employed for that purpose, as is obvious from the fact that the words dollars and units are treated as synonymous, and that all the gold coins previously described in the same section are measured by that word as the acknowledged money unit of the Constitution. Very strong doubts are entertained whether an act of Congress is absolutely necessary to constitute the gold and silver coins of the United States, fabricated and stamped as such by the proper executive officers of the mint, a legal tender in payment of debts. Constituted as such coins are by the Constitution, the standard of value, the better opinion would seem to be that they become legal tender for that purpose, if minted of the required weight and fineness, as soon as they are coined and put in circulation by lawful authority, but it is unnecessary to decide that question in this case, as the Congress, by the sixteenth section of the act establishing a mint, provided that all the gold and silver coins which shall have been struck at, and issued from, the said mint shall be a lawful tender in all payments whatsoever—those of full weight "according to the respective values herein declared, and those of less than full weight at values proportioned to their respective weights." Such a regulation is at all events highly expedient, as all experience shows that even gold and silver coins are liable to be diminished in weight by wear and abrasion, even if it is not absolutely necessary in order to constitute the coins, if of full weight, a legal tender.

Enough has already been remarked to show that the money unit of the United States is the coined dollar, described in the act establishing the mint, but if more be wanted it will be found in the twentieth section of that act, which provides that the money of account of the United States shall be expressed in dollars or units, dimes or tenths, &c., and that all accounts in the public offices and all proceedings in the federal courts shall be kept and had in conformity to that regulation.—(1 *Statutes at Large*, 248, 250.)

Completed, as the circle of measures adopted by Congress were, to put the new government into successful operation, by the passage of that act, it will be instructive to take a brief review of the important events which occurred within the period of ten years next preceding its passage, or of the ten years next following the time when that measure was first proposed in the Congress of the Confederation. Two reasons suggest the twenty-first of February, 1782, as the time to commence the review, in addition to the fact that it was on that day that the committee of Congress made their report approving of the project to establish a national mint.—(*VII. Journal of Congress*, 286.)

They are as follows: (1) Because that date just precedes the close of the war of the revolution; and, (2) Because the date at the same time extends back to a period when all America had come to the conclusion that all the paper currency in circulation was utterly worthless and that nothing was fit for a standard of value but gold and silver coin fabricated and stamped by the national authority. Discussion upon the subject was continued and the ordinance was passed, but the measure was not put in operation, as the Convention met the next year, and the Constitution was framed, adopted, and ratified, the President and the members of Congress were elected, laws were passed, the judicial system was organized, the executive departments were created, the revenue system established, and provision was made to execute the power vested in Congress to coin money and provide a standard of value, as ordained by the Constitution.

Perfect consistency characterizes the measures of that entire period in respect to the matter in question, and it would be strange if it had been otherwise, as the whole series of measures were to a very large extent the doings of the same class of men, whether the remark is applied to the old Congress, or the convention which framed the Constitution, or to the first and second sessions of the new Congress which passed the laws referred to and put the new system of government under the Constitution into full operation. Wise and complete as those laws were, still some difficulties arose, as the several states had not adopted the money unit of the United States, nor the money of account prescribed by the twentieth section of the act establishing the mint. Such embarrassments, however, were chiefly felt in the federal courts, and they were not of long continuance, as the several states, one after another, in pretty rapid succession, adopted the new system established by Congress, both as to the money unit and the money of account.

Virginia, December 19, 1792, re-enacted that section in the act of Congress without any material alteration, and New Hampshire, on the twentieth of February, 1794, passed a similar law.—(13 HENRY'S *Statutes* (*Va.*), 478. *Laws*, (*N. H.*) 240.) Massachusetts adopted the same provision the next year, and so did Rhode Island and South Carolina.—(2 *Laws Mass.*, 657. *Rev. Laws* (*R. I.*) *p.* 319. 5 *Stats.* (*S. C.*), 262.) Georgia concurred on the twenty-second of February, 1796, and New York on the twenty-second of January, 1797, and all the other states adopted the same regulation in the course of a few years.—(*M. & C. Dig.* (*Ga.*), 33. 3 *Laws* (*N. Y.*) *Greenl. ed.*, 363.) State concurrence was essential in those particulars to the proper working of the new system, and it was cheerfully accorded by the state legislatures without unnecessary delay.

Congress established as the money unit the coin mentioned in the Constitution, and the one which had been adopted as such seven years before in the resolve passed by the Congress of the Confederation. Dollars, and decimals of dollars, were adopted as the money of account by universal consent, as may be inferred from the unanimity exhibited by the states in following the example of Congress. Nothing remained for Congress to do to perfect the new system but to execute the power to coin money and regulate the value thereof, as it is clear that the Constitution makes no provision for a standard of value unless the power to establish it is conferred by that grant.

Power to fix the standard of weights and measures is vested in Congress by the Constitution in plain and unambiguous terms, and it was never doubted, certainly not until within a recent period, that the power conferred to coin money or to fabricate and stamp coins from gold and silver, which in the constitutional sense is the same thing, together with the power to determine the fineness, weight and denominations of the moneys coined, was intended to accomplish the same purpose as to values. Indubitably it was so understood by Congress in prescribing the various regulations contained in the act establishing the national mint, and it continued to be so understood by all branches of the government—executive, legislative, and judicial—

and by the whole people of the United States, for the period of seventy years, from the passage of that act.

New regulations became necessary, and were passed in the meantime increasing slightly the proportion of alloy used in fabricating the gold coins, but if those enactments are carefully examined it will be found that no one of them contains anything inconsistent in principle with the views here expressed. Gold, at the time the act establishing the mint became a law, was valued fifteen to one as compared with silver, but the disparity in value gradually increased, and to such an extent that the gold coins began to disappear from circulation, and to remedy that evil Congress found it necessary to augment the *relative* proportion of alloy by diminishing the required amount of gold whether pure or standard. Eagles coined under that act were re, quired to contain each two hundred and thirty-two grains of pure gold, or two hundred and fifty-eight grains of standard gold.—(4 *Statutes at Large*, 699.)

Three years later Congress enacted that the standard for both gold and silver coins should thereafter be such that, of one thousand parts by weight, nine hundred should be of pure metal and one hundred of alloy, by which the gross weight of the dollar was reduced to four hundred and twelve and one-half grains, but the fineness of the coins was correspondingly increased, so that the money unit remained or the same intrinsic value as under the original act. Apply that rule to the eagle and it will be seen that its gross weight would be increased, as it was in fact by that act, but it continued to contain, as under the preceding act, two hundred and thirty-two grains of pure gold and no more, showing conclusively that no change was made in the value of the coins.—(5 *Statutes at Large*, 137.)

Double eagles and gold dollars were authorized to be "struck and coined" at the mint, by the act of the third of March, 1849, but the standard established for other gold coins was not changed, and the provision was that the new coins should also be legal tender for their coined value.—(9 *Statutes at Large*, 397.)

Fractional silver coins were somewhat reduced in value by the act of the twenty-first of February, 1853, but the same act provided to the effect that the silver coins issued in conformity thereto should not be a legal tender for any sum exceeding five dollars, showing that the purpose of the enactment was to prevent the fractional coins, so essential for daily use, from being hoarded or otherwise withdrawn from circulation.—(10 *Statutes at Large*, 160.)

Suppose it be conceded, however, that the effect of that act was slightly to debase the fractional silver coins struck and coined under it, still it is quite clear that the amount was too inconsiderable to furnish any solid argument against the proposition that the standard of value in the United States was fixed by the Constitution and that such was the understanding, both of the government and of the people of the United States, for a period of more than seventy years from the time the Constitution was adopted and put in successful operation under the laws of Congress. Throughout that period the value of the money unit was never diminished, and it remains to-day, in respect to value, what it was when it was defined in the act establishing the mint, and it is safe to affirm that no one of the changes made in the other coins, except the fractional silver coins, ever extended one whit beyond the appropriate limit of constitutional regulation.

Treasury notes, called United States notes, were authorized to be issued by the act of the twenty-fifth of February, 1862, to the amount of one hundred and fifty millions of dollars, on the credit of the United States, but they were not to bear interest and were to be made payable to bearer at the treasury. They were to be issued by the Secretary of the Treasury, and the further provision was that the notes so issued should be lawful money and legal tender in payment of all debts, public and private, within the United States, except duties on imports and interest upon bonds and notes of the United States, which the act provides "shall be paid in coin."—(12 *Statutes at Large,* 345.)

Subsequent acts passed for a similar purpose also except "certificates of indebtedness and of deposit," but it will not be necessary to refer specially to the other acts as the history of that legislation is fully given in the prior decision of this court upon the same subject.— (HEPBURN *vs.* GRISWOLD, 8 *Wallace,* 618. 12 *Statutes at Large,* 370, 532, 710, 822.)

Strictly examined it is doubtful whether either of the cases before the court present any such questions as those which have been discussed in the opinion of the majority of the court just read, but suppose they do, which is not admitted, it then becomes necessary to inquire in the first place whether those questions are not closed by the recorded decisions of this court. Two questions are examined in the opinion of the majority of the court: (1) Whether the legal-tender acts are constitutional as to contracts made before the acts were passed. (2) Whether they are valid if applied to contracts made since their passage.

Assume that the views here expressed are correct and it matters not whether the contract was made before or after the act of Congress was passed, as it necessarily follows that Congress cannot, under any circumstances, make paper promises, of any kind, a legal tender in payment of debts. Prior to the decision just pronounced it is conceded that the second question presented in the record was never determined by this court, except as it is involved in the first question, but it is admitted by the majority of the court that the first question, that is the question whether the acts under consideration are constitutional as to contracts made before their passage, was fully presented in the case of HEPBURN *vs.* GRISWOLD, 8 *Wallace,* 603, and that the court decided that an act of Congress making mere paper promises to pay dollars a legal tender in payment of debts previously contracted is unconstitutional and void.

Admitted or not, it is as clear as anything in legal decision can be that the judgment of the court in that case controls the first question presented in the cases before the court, unless it be held that the judgment in that case was given for the wrong party and that the opinion given by the Chief Justice ought to be overruled.

Attempt is made to show that the second question is an open one, but the two, in my judgment, involve the same considerations, as Congress possesses no other power upon the subject than that which is derived from the grant to coin money, regulate the value thereof and of foreign coin. By that remark it is not meant to deny the proposition that Congress in executing the express grants may not pass all laws which shall be necessary and proper for carrying the same into execution, as provided in another clause of the same section of the Constitution. Much consideration of that topic is not required, as the discussion was pretty nearly exhausted by the Chief Justice in the former case, which arose under the same act and in which he gave the opinion.—(HEPBURN *vs.* GRISWOLD, 8 *Wallace,* 614, 625.)

In that case the contract bore date prior to the passage of the law, and he showed conclusively that it could never be necessary and proper, within the meaning of the Constitution, that Congress, in executing any of the express powers, should pass laws to compel a creditor to accept paper promises as fulfilling a contract for the payment of money expressed in dollars. Obviously the decision was confined to the case before the court, but I am of the opinion that the same rule must be applied whether the contract was made before or after the passage of the law, as the contract for the payment of money, expressed in dollars, is a contract to make the payment in such money as the Constitution recognizes and establishes as a standard of value. Money values can no more be measured without a standard of value than distances without a standard of extent, or quantities without a standard of weights or measures, and it is as necessary that there should be a money unit as that there should be a unit of extent, or of weight, or quantity.—(7 *Jefferson's Works,* 472. 22 *Financial Pamph.,* 417. *Horner's Bullion Report.*)

Credit currency, whether issued by the States or the United States, or by private corporations or individuals, is not recognized by the Constitution as a standard of value, nor can it be made such by any law which Congress or the States can pass, as the laws of trade are stronger than any legislative enactment. Commerce requires a standard of value and all experience warrants the prediction that commerce will have it, whether the United States agree or disagree, as the laws of commerce in that respect are stronger than the laws of any single nation of the commercial world.—(*McCulloch Commercial Dictionary,* (ed. 1869), 330.)

Values cannot be measured without a standard any more than time or duration, or length, surface or solidity, or weight, gravity, or quantity. Something in every such case must be adopted as a unit which bears a known relation to that which is to be measured, as the dollar for values, the hour for time or duration, the foot of twelve inches for length, the yard for cloth measure, the square foot or yard for surface, the cubic foot for solidity, the gallon for liquids, and the pound for weights; the pound avoirdupois being used in most commercial transactions and the pound troy " for weighing gold and silver and precious stones, except diamonds."—(2 *Bouvier Dictionary*, 648. 7 *Jefferson's Works*, 473. 1 *Jeff. Corr.*, 133.

Unrestricted power " to fix the standard of weights and measures " is vested in Congress, but until recently Congress had not enacted any general regulations in execution of that power.—(4 *Statutes at Large*, 278 5 *Ibid.*, 133. 14 *Ibid.*, 339.)

Regulations upon the subject existed in the States at the adoption of the Constitution, the same as those which prevailed at that time in the parent country, and Judge STORY says that the understanding was that those regulations remained in full force and that the States, until Congress should legislate, possessed the power to fix their own weights and measures.—(2 *Story on Constitution*, (3d ed.) sec. 1122. *Rawle on Constitution*, 102. *Cooley on Constitution*, 596. *Pomeroy on Constitution*, 263.)

Power to coin money and regulate the value of domestic and foreign coin was vested in the national government to produce uniformity of value and to prevent the embarrassments of a perpetually fluctuating and variable currency.—(2 *Story on Constitution, sec.* 1122.)

Money, says the same commentator, is the universal medium *or common standard* by a comparison with which the value of all merchandise may be ascertained; and he also speaks of it as "a sign which represents the respective values of all other commodities."— (2 *Story on Constitution, sec.* 1118.)

Such a power, that is the power to coin money, he adds, is one of the ordinary prerogatives of sovereignty, and is almost universally exercised in order to preserve a proper circulation of good coin, of a known value, in the home market.—(*Mill, Political Economy*, 294.)

Interests of such magnitude and pervading importance as those involved in providing for a uniform standard of value throughout the Union were manifestly entitled to the protection of the national authority, and in view of the evils experienced for the want of such a standard during the war of the revolution, when the country was inundated with floods of depreciated paper, the members of the convention who framed the Constitution did not hesitate to confide the power to Congress not only to coin money and regulate the value thereof, but also the power to regulate the value of foreign coin, which was denied to the Congress of the Confederation.—(2 *Phillip Paper Currency*, 135. 9 *Jefferson's Works*, 254, 289. 6 *Sparks' Washington Letters*, 321.)

Influenced by these considerations and others expressed in the opinion of the Chief Justice, this court decided in the case referred to, that the act of Congress making the notes in question "lawful money and a legal tender in payment of debts" could not be vindicated as necessary and proper means for carrying into effect the power vested in Congress to coin money and regulate the value thereof, or any other express power vested in Congress under the Constitution. Unless that case, therefore, is overruled, it is clear in my judgment, that both the cases before the court are controlled by that decision.

Controversies determined by the Supreme Court are finally and conclusively settled, as the decisions are numerous that the court cannot review and reverse their own judgments.—SIBBALD. *vs.* U. S., 12 *Peters,* 492. BRIDGE CO. *vs.* STEWART, 3 *Howard,* 424. PECK *vs.* SANDERSON, 18 *Howard,* 42. NOONAN *vs.* BRADLEY, 12 *Wallace.*)

But where the parties are different it is said the court, in a subsequent case, may overrule a former decision, and it must be admitted that the proposition in a technical point of view, is correct. Such examples are to be found in the reported decisions of the court, but they are not numerous, and it seems clear that the number ought never to be increased, especially in a matter of so much importance, unless the error is plain and upon the clearest convictions of judicial duty.

Judgment was rendered for the plaintiff in that case on the seventeenth of September, 1864, in the highest court of the state, and on the twenty-third of June, in the succeeding year, the defendants sued out a writ of error, and removed the cause into this court for re-examination.—(GRISWOLD *vs.* HEPBURN, 2 *Duvall R.*, 20.)

Under the regular call of the docket the case was first argued at the December term, 1867, but at the suggestion of the Attorney-General an order was passed that it be re-argued, and the case was accordingly continued for that purpose. Able counsel appeared at the next term, and it was again elaborately argued on both sides. Four or five other cases were also on the calendar, supposed at the time to involve the same constitutional questions, and those were also argued, bringing to the aid of the court an unusual array of counsel of great learning and eminent abilities. Investigation and deliberation followed, authorities were examined, and oft-repeated consultations among the justices ensued, and the case was held under advisement as long as necessary to the fullest examination by all the justices of the court, before the opinion of the court was delivered. By law the Supreme Court at that time consisted of the Chief Justice and seven associate justices, the act of Congress having provided that no vacancy in the office of associate justice should be filled until the number should be reduced to six.—(14 *Statutes at Large,* 209.)

Five of the number, including the Chief Justice, concurred in the opinion in that case, and the judgment of the state court was affirmed, three of the associate justices dissenting. Since that time one of the justices who concurred in that opinion of the court has resigned, and Congress having increased the number of the associate justices to eight, the two cases before the court have been argued, and the result is that the opinion delivered in the former case is overruled, five justices concurring in the present opinion and four dissenting. Five justices concurred in the first opinion, and five have overruled it.—(16 *Statutes at Large.* 44.)

Persuaded that the first opinion was right, for the reasons already assigned, it is not possible that I should concur in the second, even if it were true that no other reasons of any weight could be given in support of the judgment in the first case, and that the conclusion there reached must stand or fall without any other support. Many other reasons, however, may be invoked to fortify that conclusion, equally persuasive and convincing with those to which reference has been made.

All writers upon political economy agree that money is the universal standard of value, and the measure of exchange, foreign and domestic, and that the power to coin and regulate the value of money is an essential attribute of national sovereignty. Goods and chattels were directly bartered, one for another, when the division of labor was first introduced, but gold and silver were adopted to serve the purpose of exchange by the tacit concurrence of all nations at a very early period in the history of commercial transactions.—(*Walker, Science of Wealth*, 127.)

Commodities of various kinds were used as money at different periods in different countries, but experience soon showed the commercial nations that gold and silver embodied the qualities desirable in money in a much greater degree than any other known commodity or substance.—(1 *Smith's Wealth of Nations*, 35.)

Daily experience shows the truth of that proposition and supersedes the necessity of any remarks to enforce it, as all admit that a commodity to serve as a standard of value and a medium of exchange must be easily divisible into small portions; that it must admit of being kept for an indefinite period without deteriorating; that it must possess great value in small bulk, and be capable of being easily transported from place to place; that a given denomination of money should always be equal in weight and quality or fineness to other pieces of money of the same denomination, and that its value should be the same or as little subject to variation as possible.—(*McCulloch Com. Dic.* (ed 1869), 894. *Mill's Political Economy*, 294. 7 *Jefferson's Works*, 490.)

Such qualities, all agree, are united in a much greater degree in gold and silver than in any other known commodity, which was as well known to the members of the convention who framed the Constitution as to any body of men since assembled and entrusted to any extent with the public affairs. They not only knew that the money of the commercial world was gold and silver, but they also knew, from bitter experience, that paper promises, whether issued by the states or the United States, were utterly worthless as a standard for value for any practical purpose.

Evidence of the truth of those remarks, of the most convincing character, is to be found in the published proceedings of that convention. Debate upon the subject first arose when an amendment was proposed to prohibit the states from emitting bills of credit or making anything but gold and silver coin a tender in payment of debts, and from the character of that debate, and the vote on the amendment, it became apparent that paper money had but few, if any, friends in the convention.—(3 *Madison Papers*, 1,442.)

Article seven of the draft of the Constitution, as reported to the convention, contained the clause, " and emit bills on the credit of the

United States," appended to the grant of power vested in Congress to borrow money, and it was on the motion to strike out that clause that the principle discussion in respect to paper money took place. Mr. MADISON inquired if it would not be sufficient to prohibit the making such bills a tender, as that would remove the temptation to emit them with unjust views. Promissory notes, he said, in that shape, that is when not a tender, " may in some emergencies be best." Some were willing to acquiesce in the modification suggested by Mr. MADISON, but Mr. MORRIS, who submitted the motion, objected, insisting that if the motion prevailed there would still be room left for the notes of a responsible minister, which, as he said, " would do all the good without the mischief."

Decided objections were advanced by Mr. ELLSWORTH, who said he thought the moment a favorable one " to shut and bar the door against paper money;" and others expressed their opposition to the clause in equally decisive language, even saying that they would sooner see the whole plan rejected than retain the three words, " and emit bills." Suffice it to say, without reproducing the discussion, that the motion prevailed—nine states to two—and the clause was stricken out and no attempt was ever made to restore it.

Paper money, as legal tender, had few or no advocates in the convention, and it never had more than one open advocate throughout the period the Constitution was under discussion, either in the convention which framed it, or in the conventions of the states where it was ratified. Virginia voted in the affirmative on the motion to strike out that clause, Mr. MADISON being satisfied that if the motion prevailed it would not have the effect to disable the government from the use of treasury notes, and being himself in favor of cutting " *off the pretext for a paper currency, and particularly for making the bills a tender, either for public or private debts.*"—(3 *Madison Papers*, 1,344. 5 *Elliott's Debates*, 434, 485.)

When the draft for the Constitution was reported the clause prohibiting the states from making anything but gold and silver a tender in payment of debts contained an exception, "in case Congress consented," but the convention struck out the exception and made the prohibition absolute, one of the members remarking that it was a favorable moment to crush out paper money, and all or nearly all of the convention seemed to concur in the sentiment.—(2 *Curtis' History Constitution*, 364.)

Contemporaneous acts are certainly evidence of intention, and if so, it is difficult to see what more is needed to show that the members of that convention intended to withhold from the states, and from the United States, all power to make anything but gold and silver a standard of value, or a tender in payment of debts. Equally decisive proof to the same effect is found in the debates which subsequently occurred in the conventions of the several states, to which the Constitution, as adopted, was submitted for ratification.—(1 *Elliott's Debates*, 492. 2 *Ibid.*, 486. 4 *Ibid.*, 184. 4 *Ibid.*, 334, 336. 3 *Ibid.*, 290, 472, 478. 1 *Ibid.*, 369–370.)

Mr. MARTIN thought that the States ought not to be totally deprived of the right to emit bills of credit, but he says "that the convention was so smitten with the paper money dread that they insisted that the prohibition should be absolute."—(1 *Ibid.*, 376.)

Currency is a word much more comprehensive than the word money, as it may include bank bills and even bills of exchange as well as coins of gold and silver, but the word money, as employed in the grant of power under consideration, means the coins of gold and silver fabricated and stamped as required by law, which, by virtue of their intrinsic value, as universally acknowledged, and their official origin, become the medium of exchange and the standard by which all other values are expressed and discharged. Support to the proposition that the word money, as employed in that clause, was intended to be used in the sense here supposed is also derived from the language employed in certain numbers of the *Federalist*, which, as is well known, were written and published during the period the question whether the states would ratify the Constitution was pending in their several conventions. Such men as the writers of those essays never could have employed such language if they had entertained the remotest idea that Congress possessed the power to make paper promises a legal tender.—(*Federalist*, No. 44, p. 207. *Ibid.*, No. 42, p. 197.)

Like support is also derived from the language of Mr. HAMILTON in his celebrated report recommending the incorporation of a national bank. He first states the objection to the proposed measure, that banks tend to banish the gold and silver of the country; and secondly he gives the answer to that objection made by the advocates of the bank, that it is immaterial what serves the purpose of money, and then says that the answer is not entirely satisfactory, as the permanent increase or decrease of the precious metals in a country can hardly ever be a matter of indifference. "As the commodity taken in lieu of every other, it (coin) is a species of the most effective wealth, and as the money of the world it is of great concern to the state that it possesses a sufficiency of it to face any demands which the protection of its external interests may create." He favored the incorporation of a national bank, with power to issue bills and notes *payable on demand in gold and silver*, but he expressed himself as utterly opposed to paper emissions by the United States, characterizing them as so liable to abuse and even so certain of being abused that the government ought never to trust itself "with the use of so seducing and dangerous an element.—(*Clarke's History U. S. Bank*, 21, 24, 32.)

Opposed as he was to paper emissions by the United States, under any circumstances, it is past belief that he could ever have concurred in the proposition to make such emissions a tender in payment of debts, either as a member of the convention which framed the Constitution or as the head of the Treasury Department. Treasury notes, however, have repeatedly been authorized by Congress, commencing with the act of the thirtieth of June, 1812, but it was never supposed before the time when the several acts in question were passed that Congress could make such notes a legal tender in payment of debts.— (2 *Statutes at Large*, 766. 3 *Ibid.* 100.)

Such notes, it was enacted, should be received in payment of all duties and taxes laid, and in payment for public lands sold, by the federal authority Provision was also made in one or more of the acts that the Secretary of the Treasury, with the approbation of the President, might cause treasury notes to be issued, at the par value thereof, in payment of services, of supplies, or of debts for which the United States were or might be answerable by law, to such person or persons as should be *willing to accept the same* in payment, but it never occurred to the legislators of that day that such notes could be made a legal tender in discharge of such indebtedness, or that the public creditor could be compelled to accept them in payment of his just demands.—(3 *Ibid.*, 315.)

Financial embarrassments, second only, in their disastrous consequences, to those which preceded the adoption of the Constitution, arose towards the close of the last war with Great Britain, and it is matter of history that those embarrassments were too great and pervading to be overcome by the use of treasury notes or any other paper emissions without a specie basis. Expedients of various kinds were suggested, but it never occurred either to the executive or to Congress that a remedy could be found by making treasury notes, as then authorized, a legal tender, and the result was that the second bank of the United States was incorporated.—(3 *Ibid.*, 266.)

Paper currency, it may be said, was authorized by that act, which is undoubtedly true; and it is also true that the bills or notes of the bank were made receivable in all payments to the United States, if the same were at the time payable on demand, but the act provided that the corporation should not refuse, under a heavy penalty, the payment in gold and silver, of any of its notes, bills, or obligations, nor of any moneys received upon deposit in the bank or in any of its offices of discount and deposit.

Serious attempt is made, strange to say, to fortify the proposition that the acts in question are constitutional, from the fact that Congress, in providing for the use of treasury notes, and in granting the charters to the respective national banks, made the notes and bills receivable in payment of duties and taxes, but the answer to the suggestion is so obvious, that it is hardly necessary to pause to suggest its refutation.—(METROPOLITAN BANK *vs.* VAN DYCK, 27 *N. Y.*, 42.)

Creditors may exact gold and silver or they may waive the right to require such money, and accept credit currency, or commodities, other than gold and silver, and the United States, as creditors, or in the exercise of their express power to lay and collect taxes, duties, imposts and excises, may, if they see fit, accept the treasury notes or bank bills in such payments as substitutes for the constitutional currency. Further discussion of the proposition is unnecessary, as it is plainly destitute of any merit whatever.—(4 *Webster's Works*, 271. THORNDIKE *vs.* UNITED STATES, 2 *Mason*, 18.)

Resort was also had to treasury notes in the revulsion of 1837, and during the war with Mexico, and also in the great revulsion of 1857, but the new theory that Congress could make treasury notes a legal tender was not even suggested, either by the President or by any member of Congress.—(5 *Statutes at Large*, 201. 5 *Ibid.*, 469. 9 *Ibid.*, 118. 11 *Ibid.*, 257.)

Seventy years are included in this review, even if the computation is only carried back to the passage of the act establishing the mint, and it is clear that there is no trace of any act, executive or legislative, within that period, which affords the slightest support to the new constitutional theory that Congress can by law constitute paper emissions a tender in payment of debts. Even WASHINGTON, the father of our country, refused to accept paper money in payment of debts contracted before the war of independence, and the proof is full to the point that HAMILTON, as well as JEFFERSON and MADISON, was opposed to paper emissions by the national authority.—(2 *Phillips' Paper Currency*, 135. 6 *Sparks' Washington Letters*, 321.)

Sufficient, also, is recorded in the reports of the decisions of this court to show that the court, from the organization of the judicial system to the day when the judgments in the cases before the court were announced, held opinions utterly opposed to such a construction of the Constitution as would authorize Congress to make paper promises a legal tender as between debtor and creditor.—(*Legal-Tender Cases*, 11 *Wallace*, 682.)

Throughout that period the doctrine of the court has been, and still is, unless the opinion of the court just read constitutes an exception, that the government of the United States, as ordained or established by the Constitution, is a government of enumerated powers ; that all the powers not delegated to the United States by the Constitution nor prohibited by it to the States, are reserved to the States respectively or to the people; that every power vested in the federal government under the Constitution is in its nature sovereign, and that Congress may pass all laws necessary and proper to carry the same into execution, or, in other words, that the power being sovereign includes, by force of the term, the requisite means, fairly applicable to the attainment of the contemplated end, which are not precluded by restrictions or exceptions expressed or necessarily implied and not contrary to the essential ends of political society.—(*History U. S. Bank*, 95.)

Definitions slightly different have been given by different jurists to the words "necessary and proper" employed in the clause of the Constitution conferring upon Congress the power to pass laws for carrying the express grants of power into execution, but no one ever pretended that a construction or definition could be sustained that the general clause would authorize the employment of such means in the execution of one express grant as would practically nullify another, or render another utterly nugatory. Circumstances made it necessary that Mr. HAMILTON should examine that phrase at a very early period after the Constitution was adopted, and the definition he gave to it is as follows : " All the means requisite and fairly applicable to the attainment of the end of such power which are not precluded by restrictions and exceptions specified in the Constitution, and not contrary to the essential ends of political society." Twenty-five years later the question was examined by the Supreme Court and authoritatively settled, the Chief Justice giving the opinion. His words were: " Let the end be legitimate, let it be within the scope of the Constitution, and all means which are appropriate, which are plainly adapted to that end, and which are not prohibited but consistent with the letter and spirit of the Constitution, are constitutional."—(McCULLOH *vs.* MARYLAND, 4 *Wheaton*, 421.)

Substantially the same definition was adopted by the present Chief Justice in the former case, in which he gave the opinion of the court, and there is nothing contained in the federal reports giving the slightest sanction to any broader definition of those words. Take the definition given by Mr. HAMILTON, which, perhaps, is the broadest, if there is any difference, and still it is obvious that it would give no countenance whatever to the theory that Congress, in passing a law to execute one express grant of the Constitution, could authorize means which would nullify another express grant, or render it nugatory for the attainment of the end which the framers of the Constitution intended it should accomplish.

Authority to coin money was vested in Congress to provide a permanent national standard of value, everywhere the same and subject to no variation except what Congress shall make under the power to regulate the value thereof, and it is not possible to affirm, with any hope that the utterance will avail in the argument, that the power to coin money is not an express power, and if those premises are conceded it cannot be shown that Congress can so expand any other express power by implication as to nullify or defeat the great purposes which the power to coin money and establish a standard of value was intended to accomplish.

Government notes, it is conceded, may be issued as a means of borrowing money, because the act of issuing the notes may be, and often is, a requisite means to execute the granted power, and being fairly applicable to the attainment of the end, the notes, as means, may be employed, as they are not precluded by any restrictions or exceptions and are not repugnant to any other express grant contained in the Constitution. Light-houses, buoys, and beacons may be erected under the power to regulate commerce, but Congress cannot authorize an officer of the government to take private property for such a purpose without just compensation, as the exercise of such a power would be repugnant to the fifth amendment. Power to lay and collect taxes is conferred upon Congress, but the Congress cannot tax the salaries of the state judges, as the exercise of such a power is incompatible with the admitted power of the states to create courts, appoint judges, and provide for their compensation.—(COLLECTOR *vs.* DAY, 11 *Wallace.* 113. WARD *vs.* MARYLAND, 12 *Wallace.*)

Congress may also impose duties, imposts, and excises to pay the debts and provide for the common defence and general welfare, but the Congress cannot lay any tax or duty on articles exported from any state, nor can Congress give any preference by any regulation of commerce or revenue to the ports of one state over those of another, as the exercise of any such power is prohibited by the Constitution. Exclusive power is vested in Congress to declare war, to raise and support armies, to provide and maintain a navy, and to make rules for the government and regulation of the land and naval forces. Appropriations to execute those powers may be made by Congress, but no appropriations of money to that use can be made for a longer term than two years, as an appropriation for a longer term is expressly prohibited by the same clause which confers the power to raise and support armies. By virtue of those grants of power Congress may erect forts and magazines, may construct navy-yards and dock-yards, manufacture arms and munitions of war, and may establish depots and other needful buildings for their preservation, but the Congress cannot take private property for that purpose without making compensation to the owner, as the Constitution provides that private property shall not be taken for public use without just compensation.

Legislative power under the Constitution can never be rightfully extended to the exercise of a power not granted nor to that which is prohibited, and it makes no difference whether the prohibition is express or implied, as an implied prohibition, when once ascertained, is as effectual to negative the right to legislate as one that is expressed; the rule being that Congress, in passing laws to carry the express powers granted into execution, cannot select any means as requisite for that purpose or as fairly applicable to the attainment of the end which are precluded by restrictions or exceptions contained in the Constitution, or which are contrary to the essential ends of political society.—(*History Bank U. S.*, 95.)

Concede these premises, and it follows that the acts of Congress in question cannot be regarded as valid unless it can be held that the power to make paper emissions a legal tender in payment of debts can properly be implied from the power to coin money, and that such emissions, when enforced by such a provision, become the legal standard of value under the Constitution. Extended discussion of the first branch of the proposition would seem to be unnecessary, as the dissenting justices in the former case abandoned that point, and frankly stated in the dissenting opinion delivered that they were not able to see in those clauses, "standing alone, a sufficient warrant for the exercise of this power."

Through their organ on the occasion they referred to the power to declare war, to suppress insurrection, to raise and support armies, to provide and maintain a navy, to borrow money, to pay the debts of the Union, and to provide for the common defence and general welfare, as grants of power conferred in separate clauses of the Constitution. Reference was then made in very appropriate terms to the exigencies of the treasury during that period, and the conclusion reached, though expressed interrogatively, appears to be that the provision making the notes a legal tender was a necessary and proper one as conducing "towards the purpose of borrowing money, of paying debts, of raising armies, of suppressing insurrection," or, as expressed in another part of the same opinion, the provision was regarded as

" necessary and proper to enable the government to borrow money to carry on the war."—(HEPBURN *vs.* GRISWOLD, 8 *Wallace*, 632.)

Suggestions or intimations are made in one or more of the opinions given in the state courts that the power assumed by Congress may be vindicated as properly implied from the power to coin money, but inasmuch as that assumption was not the ground of the dissent in the former case, and as the court is not referred to any case where a court affirming the validity of the acts of Congress in question has ventured to rest their decision upon that theory, it does not appear to be necessary to protract the discussion upon that point.

Such notes are not declared in the acts of Congress to be a standard of value, and if they were the provision would be as powerless to impart that quality to the notes as were the processes of the alchemist to convert chalk into gold, or the contrivances of the mechanic to organize a machine and give it perpetual motion. Gold and silver were adopted as the standard of value, even before civil governments were organized, and they have always been regarded as such to the present time, and it is safe to affirm that they will continue to be such by universal consent, in spite of legislative enactments and of judicial decisions. Treasury notes, or the notes in question, called by what name they may be, never performed that office, even for a day, and it may be added that neither legislative enactments nor judicial decisions can compel the commercial world to accept paper emissions of any kind as the standard of value by which all other values are to be measured.—(HEPBURN *vs.* GRISWOLD, 8 *Wallace*, 608.)

Nothing but money will in fact perform that office, and it is clear that neither legislative enactments nor judicial decisions can perform commercial impossibilities. Commodities undoubtedly may be exchanged as matter of barter, or the seller may accept paper promises instead of money, but it is nevertheless true, as stated by MR. HUSKISSON, that money is not only the *common measure* and *common representative* of all other commodities, but also the common and universal equivalent. Whoever buys, gives, whoever sells, receives such a quantity of pure gold or silver as is equivalent to the article bought or sold ; or if he gives or receives paper instead of money, he gives or receives that which is valuable only as it stipulates the payment of a given quantity of gold or silver.—(22 *Financial Pamphlets*, 580.)

Most unquestionably, said Mr. WEBSTER, there is no legal tender, and there can be no legal tender, in this country, under the authority of this government, or any other, but gold and silver. * * This is a constitutional principle, perfectly plain and of the very highest importance. He admitted that no such express prohibition was contained in the Constitution, and then proceeded to say, "as Congress has no power granted to it in this respect but to coin money and to regulate the value of foreign coins, *it clearly has no power to substitute paper* or any thing else for coin as a tender in payment of debts and in discharge of contracts," adding that " Congress has exercised the power fully in both its branches. It has coined money and still coins it, it has regulated the value of foreign coins and still regulates their value. The legal tender, therefore, THE CONSTITUTIONAL STANDARD

OF VALUE, IS ESTABLISHED AND CANNOT BE OVERTHROWN."—(4 Webster's Works, 271.)

Beyond peradventure he was of the opinion that gold and silver, at rates fixed by Congress, constituted the legal standard of value, and that neither Congress nor the states had authority to establish any other standard in its place.—(4 *Ibid.*, 280.)

Views equally decisive have been expressed by this court in a case where the remarks were pertinent to the question presented for decision.—(U. S. *vs.* MARIGOLD, 9 *Howard*, 567.)

Certain questions were certified here which arose in the circuit court in the trial of an indictment in which the defendant was charged with having brought into the United States from a foreign place, with intent to pass, utter, publish, and sell certain false, forged, and counterfeit coins, made, forged, and counterfeited in the resemblance and similitude of the coins struck at the mint. Doubts were raised at the trial whether Congress had the power to pass the law on which the indictment was found. Objection was made that the acts charged were only a fraud in traffic, and, as such, were punishable, if at all, under the state law. Responsive to that suggestion the court say that the provisions of the section "appertain rather to the execution of an important trust invested by the Constitution, and to the obligation to fulfill that trust on the part of the government, namely, the trust and the duty of creating and maintaining *a uniform and pure metallic standard of value throughout the Union;* that the power of coining money and of regulationg its value was delegated to Congress by the Constitution for the very purpose of *creating and preserving the uniformity and purity of such a standard of value,* and on account of the impossibility which was foreseen of otherwise preventing the inequalities and the confusion necessarily incident to different views of policy which in different communities would be brought to bear on this subject. The power to coin money being thus given to Congress, founded on public necessity, it must carry with it the correlative power of protracting the creature and object of that power."

Appropriate suggestions follow as to the right of the government to adopt measures to exclude counterfeits and prevent the true coin from being substituted by others of no intrinsic value, and the justice delivering the opinion then proceeds to say, that Congress "having emitted a circulating medium, *a standard of value indispensable for the purposes of the community* and for the action of the government itself, the Congress is accordingly authorized and bound in duty to prevent its debasement and expulsion and the destruction of the general confidence and convenience by the influx and substitution of a spurious coin in lieu of the constitutional currency." Equally decisive views were expressed by the court six years earlier, in the case of GWIN *vs.* BREEDLOVE, (2 *Howard*, 38,) in which the opinion of the court was delivered by the late Mr. Justice CATRON, than whom no justice who ever sat in the court was more opposed to the expression of an opinion on a point not involved in the record.

No state shall coin money, emit bills of credit, or make anything but gold and silver a tender in payment of debts. These prohibitions, said Mr. Justice WASHINGTON, associated with the powers granted to Congress to coin money and regulate the value thereof and of foreign coin, most obviously constitute members of the same family, being upon the same subject and governed by the same policy. This policy, said the learned justice, was to provide a fixed and uniform standard of value throughout the United States by which the commercial and other dealings between the citizens thereof, or between them and foreigners, as well as the moneyed transactions of the government, should be regulated.—(OGDEN *vs.* SAUNDERS, 12 *Wheaton*, 265.)

Language so well chosen and so explicit cannot be misunderstood, and the views expressed by Mr. Justice JOHNSON in the same case are even more decisive. He said the prohibition in the Constitution to make anything but gold or silver coin a tender in payment of debts is *express and universal*. The framers of the Constitution regarded it as an evil to be repelled without modification, and that they have therefore left nothing to be inferred or deduced from construction on the subject.—(12 *Ibid.*, 288.)

Recorded as those opinions have been for forty-five years, and never questioned, they are certainly entitled to much weight, especially as the principles which are there laid down were subsequently affirmed in two cases by the unanimous opinion of this court.—(UNITED STATES *vs.* MARIGOLD, 9 *Howard*, 567. GWIN *vs.* BREEDLOVE, 2 *Howard*, 38. CRAIG *vs.* MISSOURI, 4 *Peters*, 434.)

Strong support to the view here taken is also derived from the case last cited, in which the opinion was given by the Chief Justice. Loan certificates issued by the state were the consideration of the note in suit in that case, and the defence was that the certificates were bills of credit and that the consideration of the note was illegal. Responsive to that defence the plaintiff insisted that the certificates were not bills of credit, because they had not been made a legal tender, to which the court replied, that the emission of bills of credit and the enactment of tender laws were distinct operations, independent of each other ; that both were forbidden by the Constitution; that the evils of paper money did not result solely from the quality of its being made a tender in payment of debts; that that quality might be the *most pernicious* one, but that it was not an essential quality of bills of credit nor the only mischief resulting from such emissions.—(BRISCOE *vs.* BANK OF KENTUCKY, 11 *Peters*, 317. FOX *vs.* OHIO, 5 *Howard*, 433.)

Remarks of the Chief Justice in the case of STURGES *vs.* CROWNINSHIELD, (4 *Wheaton*, 204,) may also be referred to as even more explicit and decisive to the same conclusion than anything embodied in the other cases. He first describes, in vivid colors, the general distress which followed the war in which our independence was established. Paper money, he said, was issued, worthless lands and other property of no use to the creditor were made a tender in payment of debts, and and the time of payment stipulated in the contract was extended by law. Mischief to such an extent was done, and so much more was apprehended, that general distrust prevailed and all confidence between man and man was destroyed. Special reference was made to those grievances by the Chief Justice because it was insisted that the prohibition to pass laws impairing the obligation of contracts ought to be confined by the court to matters of that description, but the court was of a different opinion, and held that the convention intended to establish a great principle, that contracts should be inviolable, that the provision was intended " to prohibit the use of any means by which the same mischief might be produced."

He admitted that that provision was not intended to prevent the issue of paper money, as that evil was remedied and the practice prohibited by the clause forbidding the states to " emit bills of credit," inserted in the Constitution expressly for that purpose, and he also admitted that the prohibition to emit bills of credit was not intended to restrain the states from enabling debtors to discharge their debts by the tender of property of no real value to the creditor, "because for that subject also particular provision is made " in the Constitution; but he added, " NOTHING BUT GOLD AND SILVER COIN CAN BE MADE A TENDER IN PAYMENT OF DEBTS,"—(STURGES vs. CROWNINSHIELD, 4 *Ibid.*, 205.)

Utterances of the kind are found throughout the reported decisions of this court, but there is not a sentence or word to be found within those volumes, from the organization of the court to the passage of the acts of Congress in question, to support the opposite theory. Power, as before remarked, was vested in the Congress under the Confederation to borrow money and emit bills of credit, and history shows that the power to emit such bills had been exercised, before the convention which framed the Constitution assembled, to an amount exceeding three hundred and fifty millions of dollars.—(2 *Story on Constitution*, 3d ed., 249. BRISCOE vs. BANK OF KENTUCKY, 11 Peters, 337. 1 *Jefferson's Correspondence*, 401. *Am. Almanac*, 1830, 183.)

Still the draft of the Constitution, as reported, contained the words " and to emit bills " appended to the clause authorizing Congress to borrow money. When that clause was reached, says Mr. MARTIN, a motion was made to strike out the words " to emit *bills of credit;*" and his account of what followed affords the most persuasive and convincing evidence that the convention, and nearly every member of it, intended to put an end to the exercise of such a power. Against the motion, he says, we urged that it would be improper to deprive the Congress of that power; that it would be a novelty unprecedented to establish a government which should not have such authority; that it was impossible to look forward into futurity so far as to decide that events might not happen that would render the exercise of such a power absolutely necessary, &c. But a majority of the convention, he said, being wise beyond every event, and being willing to risk any political evil rather than admit the idea of a paper emission *in any possible case*, refused to trust the authority to a government to which they were lavishing the most unlimited powers of taxation, and to the mercy of which they were willing blindly to trust the liberty and property of the citizens of every State in the Union, and "*they erased that clause from the system.*"—(1 *Elliott's Debates,* 369.)

More forcible vindication of the action of the convention could hardly be made than is expressed, in the language of the *Federalist,* and the authority of Judge STORY warrants the statement that the language there employed is "justified by almost every contemporary writer," and is "attested in its truth by facts" beyond the influence of every attempt at contradiction. Having adverted to those facts the commentator proceeds to say, "that the same reasons which show the necessity of denying to the states the power of regulating coin, prove with equal force that they ought not to be at liberty to substitute a paper medium instead of coin."—(*Federalist,* No. 44.)

Emissions of the kind were not declared by the Continental Congress to be a legal tender, but Congress passed a resolution declaring that they ought to be a tender in payment of all private and public debts, and that a refusal to receive a tender ought to be an extinguishment of the debt, and recommended the states to pass such laws. They even went further and declared that whoever should refuse to receive the paper as gold or silver should be deemed an enemy to the public liberty, but our commentator says that these measures of violence and terror so far from aiding the circulation of the paper led on to still further depreciation.—(2 *Journal Congress,* 21. 3 *Ibid.,* 20. 2 *Pitkin's History,* 155, 6.)

New emissions followed and new measures were adopted to give the paper credit by pledging the public faith for its redemption. Effort followed effort in that direction until the idea of redemption at par was abandoned. Forty for one was offered, and the states were required to report the bills under that regulation, but few of the old bills were ever reported, and of course few only of the contemplated new notes were issued, and the bills in a brief period ceased to circulate, and in the course of that year quietly died in the hands of their possessors.—(2 *Story on Constitution,* 3d ed., secs. 1359, 1360. 2 *Pitkin's History,* 157. 1 *Jefferson's Correspondence,* 402.)

Bills of credit were made a tender by the states, but all such, as well as those issued by the Congress, were dead in the hands of their possessors before the convention assembled to frame the Constitution. Intelligent and impartial belief in the theory that such men, so instructed, in framing a government for their posterity as well as for themselves, would deliberately vest such a power, either in Congress or the states, as a part of their perpetual system, can never in my judgment be secured in the face of the recorded evidences to the contrary which the political and judicial history of our country affords. Such evidence, so persuasive and convincing as it is, must ultimately bring all to the conclusion that neither the Congress nor the states can make anything but gold or silver coin a tender in payment of debts.

Exclusive power to coin money is certainly vested in Congress, but "no amount of reasoning can show that executing a promissory note and ordering it to be taken in payment of public and private debts is a species of coining money."—(*Pomeroy on Constitution, sec.* 409.)

Complete refutation of such theory is also found in the dissenting opinion in the former case, in which the justice who delivered the opinion states that he is not able to deduce the power to pass the laws in question from that clause of the Constitution, and in which he admits, without qualification, that the provision making such notes a legal tender does undoubtedly impair the "obligation of contracts made before its passage." Extended argument, therefore, to show that the acts in question impair the obligation of contracts made before their passage is unnecessary, but the admission stops short of the whole truth, as it leaves the implication to be drawn that the obligation of subsequent contracts is not impaired by such legislation.

Contracts for the payment of money, whether made before or after the passage of such a provision, are contracts, if the promise is expressed in dollars, to pay the specified amount in the money recognized and established by the Constitution as the standard of value, and any act of Congress which in theory compels the creditor to accept paper emissions, instead of the money so recognized and established, impairs the obligation of such a contract, no matter whether the contract was made before or after the act compelling the creditor to accept such payment, as the Constitution in that respect is a part of the contract, and by its terms entitles the creditor to demand payment in the medium which the Constitution recognizes and establishes as the standard of value.

Evidently the word dollar, as employed in the Constitution, means the money recognized and established in the express power vested in Congress to coin money, regulate the value thereof and of foreign coin, the framers of the Constitution having borrowed and adopted the word as used by the Continental Congress in the ordinance of the sixth of July, 1785, and of the eighth of August, 1786, in which it was enacted that the money unit of the United States should be "one dollar," and that the money of account should be dollars and fractions of dollars, as subsequently provided in the ordinance establishing a mint.—(10 *Journals of Congress*, 225. 11 *Ibid.*, 179.)

Repeated decisions of this court, of recent date, have established the rule that contracts to pay coined dollars can only be satisfied by the payment of such money, which is precisely equivalent to a decision that such notes as those described in the acts of Congress in question are not the money recognized and established by the Constitution as the standard of value, as the money so recognized and established, if the contract is expressed in dollars, will satisfy any and every contract between party and party.—(BRONSON *vs.* RODES, 7 *Wallace*, 248. BUTLER *vs.* HORWITZ, 7 *Wallace*, 259. BANK *vs.* SUPERVISORS, 7 *Wallace*, 28.)

Beyond all question those cases recognize "the fact, accepted by all men throughout the world, that value is inherent in the precious metals; that gold and silver are in themselves values, and being such, and being in other respects best adapted to the purpose, are *the only proper measures of value ;* that these values are determined by weight and purity, and that form and impress are simply certificates of value, worthy of absolute reliance only because of the known integrity and good faith of the government which" put them in circulation.—(DEWING *vs.* SEARS, 11 *Wallace*, 379. LANE CO. *vs.* OREGON, 7 *Wallace*, 73. WILLARD *vs.* TAYLOE, 8 *Wallace*, 568.

When the intent of the parties as to the medium of payment is clearly expressed in a contract, the court decide, in the second case above cited, that damages for the breach of it, whether made before or since the enactment of these laws, may be properly assessed so as to give effect to that intent, and no doubt is entertained that that rule is correct. Parties may contract to accept payment in treasury notes, or specific articles, or in bank bills, and if they do so they are bound to accept the medium for which they contracted, provided the notes, specific articles, or bills, are tendered on the day the payment under the contract becomes due; and it is clear that such a tender, if seasonable and sufficient in amount, is a good defence to the action. Decided cases also carry the doctrine much further, and hold, even where the contract is payable in money and the promise is expressed in dollars, that a tender of bank bills is a good tender if the party to whom it was made placed his objections to receiving it wholly upon the ground that the amount was not sufficient.—(U. S. BANK *vs.* BANK OF STATE OF GEORGIA, 10 *Wheaton*, 347. THOMPSON *vs.* RIGGS, 5 *Wallace*, 678. ROBINSON *vs.* NOBLE, 8 *Peters*, 198. WRIGHT *vs.* REID, 3 *Term*, 554. SNOW *vs.* PERRY, 9 *Pickering*, 542. 2 *Greenl. Evidence, sec.* 601.)

Grant all that, and still it is clear that where the contract is for the payment of a certain sum of money, and the promise is expressed in dollars, or in coined dollars, the promisee, if he sees fit, may lawfully refuse to accept payment in any other medium than gold and silver, made a legal tender by act of Congress passed in pursuance of that provision of the Constitution which vests in Congress the power to coin money, regulate the value thereof and of foreign coin.

Foreign coin of gold and silver may be made a legal tender, as the power to regulate the value thereof is vested in Congress as well as the power to regulate the value of the coins fabricated and stamped at the mint.

Opposed, as the new theory is, by such a body of evidence, covering the whole period of our constitutional history, all tending to the opposite conclusion, and unsupported as the theory is by a single historical fact, entitled to any weight, it would seem that the advocates of the theory ought to be able to give it a fixed domicile in the Constitution, or else be willing to abandon it as a theory without any solid constitutional foundation. Vagrancy in that behalf, if conceded, is certainly a very strong argument at this day, that the power does not reside in the Constitution at all, as if the fact were otherwise, the period of eighty-five years which has elapsed since the Constitution was adopted is surely long enough to have enabled its advocates to discover its locality, and to be able to point out its home to those whose researches have been less successful, and whose conscientious convictions lead them to the conclusion that, as applied to the Constitution, it is a myth without a habitation or a name.

Unless the power to enact such a provision can be referred to some one or more of the express grants of power to Congress, as the requisite means, or as necessary and proper for carrying such express power or powers into execution, it is usually conceded that the provision must be regarded as unconstitutional, as it is not pretended that the Constitution contains any express grant of power authorizing such legislation. Powers not granted cannot be exercised by Congress, and certainly all must agree that no powers are granted except what are expressed or such as are fairly applicable as requisite means to attain the end of a power which is granted, or, in other words, are necessary and proper to carry those which are expressed into execution.—(MARTIN *vs.* HUNTER'S LESSEE, 1 *Wheaton,* 326. MCCULLOH *vs.* MARYLAND, 4 *Wheaton,* 405. 1 *Story on Constitution,* (3d ed.,) sec. 417.)

Pressed by these irrepealable rules of construction, as applied to the Constitution, those who maintain the affirmative of the question under discussion are forced to submit a specification. Courts in one or more cases have intimated that the power in question may be implied from the express power to coin money, but inasmuch as no decided case is referred to where the judgment of the court rests upon that ground, the suggestion will be dismissed without further consideration as one involving a proposition too latitudinous to require refutation. Most of the cases referred to attempt to deduce the power to make such paper emissions a legal tender from the express power to borrow money, or from the power to declare war, or from the two combined, as in the dissenting opinion in the case which is now overruled.

Authority, it is conceded, exists in Congress to pass laws providing for the issue of treasury notes, based on the national credit, as necessary and proper means for fulfilling the end of the express power to borrow money, nor can it be doubted at this day, that such notes, when issued by the proper authority, may lawfully circulate as credit currency, and that they may, in that conventional character, be lawfully employed, if the act authorizing their issue so provides, to pay duties, taxes, and all the public exactions required to be paid into the national treasury. Public creditors may also be paid in such currency by their own consent, and they may be used in all other cases, where the payment in such notes comports with the terms of the contract.

Established usage, founded upon the practice of the government, often repeated, has sanctioned these rules, until it may now be said that they are not open to controversy, but the question in the cases before the court is whether the Congress may declare such notes to be lawful money, make them a legal tender, and impart to such a currency the quality of being a standard of value, and compel creditors to accept the payment of their debts in such a currency as the equivalent of the money recognized and established by the Constitution as the standard of value by which the value of all other commodities is to be measured.

Financial measures, of various kinds, for borrowing money to supply the wants of the treasury, beyond the receipts from taxation and the sales of the public lands, have been adopted by the government since the United States became an independent nation. Subscriptions for a loan of twelve millions of dollars were, on the fourth of August, 1790, directed to be opened at the treasury, to be made payable in certificates issued for the debt according to their specie value.—(1 *Statutes at Large*, 139.)

Measures of the kind were repeated in rapid succession for several years, and laws providing for loans in one form or another appear to have been the preferred mode of borrowing money, until the thirtieth of June, 1812, when the first act was passed " to authorize the issue of treasury notes."—(2 *Statutes at Large*, 766.)

Loans had been previously authorized in repeated instances, as will be seen by the following references, to which many more might be added. 1 *Ibid.*, 142. 1 *Ibid.*, 187. 1 *Ibid.*, 345. 1 *Ibid.*, 433. 1 *Ibid.*, 607. 2 *Ibid.*, 60. 2 *Ibid.*, 245. 2 *Ibid.*, 349. 2 *Ibid.*, 610. 2 *Ibid.*, 656. 2 *Ibid.*, 694.

Earnest opposition was made to the passage of the first act of Congress authorizing the issue of treasury notes, but the measure prevailed, and it may be remarked that the vote on the occasion was ever after regarded as having settled the question as to the constitutionality of such an act. Five millions of dollars were directed to be issued by that act, and the Secretary of the Treasury, with the approbation of the President, was empowered to cause such portion of the notes as he might deem expedient to be issued at par " to such public creditors *or other persons as may choose to receive such notes in payment;*" it never having occurred to any one that even a public creditor could be compelled to receive such notes in payment except by his own consent.

Twenty other issues of such notes were authorized by Congress in the course of the fifty years next after the passage of that act and before the passage of the acts making such notes a legal tender, and every one of such prior acts, being twenty in all, contains either in express words or by necessary implication, an equally decisive negation to the new constitutional theory that Congress can make paper emissions, either a standard of value, or a legal tender.—(5 *Ibid.*, 202. 9 *Ibid.*, 64. 4 *Ibid.*, 765. 2 *Ibid.*, 766. 2 *Ibid.*, 801. 3 *Ibid.*, 161. 3 *Ibid.*, 213. 5 *Ibid.*, 201. 5 *Ibid*, 228. 5 *Ibid.*, 323. 5 *Ibid.*, 469. 5 *Ibid.*, 474. 5 *Ibid.*, 581. 5 *Ibid.*, 614. 9 *Ibid.*, 39. 9 *Ibid.*, 118. 11 *Ibid.*, 257. 12 *Ibid.*, 121. 12 *Ibid.*, 179. 12 *Ibid.*, 259. 12 *Ibid.*, 313. 12 *Ibid.*, 338.)

Superadded to the conceded fact that the Constitution contains no express words to support such a theory, this long and unbroken usage, that treasury notes shall not be constituted a standard of value nor be made a tender in payment of debts, is entitled to great weight, and when taken in connection with the persuasive and convincing evidence, derived from the published proceedings of the convention, that the framers of the Constitution never intended to grant any such power, and from the recorded sentiments of the great men whose arguments in favor of the reported draft procured its ratification, and supported as that view is by the repeated decisions of this court, and by the infallible rule of interpretation that the language of one express power shall not be so expanded as to nullify the force and effect of another express power in the same instrument, it seems to me that it ought to be deemed final and conclusive that Congress cannot constitute such notes, or any other paper emissions, a constitutional standard of value, or make them a legal tender in payment of debts—especially as it covers the period of two foreign wars, the creation of the second national bank, and the greatest financial revulsions through which our country has ever passed.

Guided by the views expressed in the dissenting opinion in the former case it must be taken for granted that the legal-tender feature in the acts in question was placed emphatically, by those who enacted the provision, upon the necessity of the measure to the further borrowing of money and maintaining the army and navy, and such appears to be the principal ground assumed in the present opinion of the court. Enough also appears in some of the interrogative sentences of the dissenting opinion to show that the learned justice who delivered it intended to place the dissent very largely upon the same ground.

Nothing need be added, it would seem, to show that the power to make such notes a standard of value and a legal tender cannot be derived from the power to borrow money, without so expanding it by implication as to nullify the power to coin money and regulate its value, nor without extending the scope and operation of the power to borrow money to an object never contemplated by the framers of the Constitution; and if so, then it only remains to enquire whether it may be implied from the power to declare war, to raise and support armies, or to provide and maintain a navy, or "to enable the government to borrow money to carry on the war," as the phrase is in the dissenting opinion in the former case.

Money is undoubtedly the sinews of war, but the power to raise money to carry on war, under the Constitution, is not an implied power, and whoever adopts that theory commits a great constitutional error. Congress may declare war and Congress may appropriate all moneys in the treasury to carry on the war, or Congress may coin money for that purpose or borrow money to any amount for the same purpose, or Congress may lay and collect taxes, duties, imposts, and excises to replenish the treasury, or may dispose of the public lands or other property belonging to the United States, and may in fact, by the exercise of the express powers of the Constitution, command the whole wealth and substance of the people to sustain the public credit, and prosecute the war to a successful termination.

Two foreign wars were successfully conducted by means derived from those sources, and it is not doubted that those express powers will always enable Congress to maintain the national credit and defray the public expenses in every emergency which may arise, even though the national independence should be assailed by the combined forces of all the rest of the civilized world. All remarks, therefore, in the nature of entreaty or appeal, in favor of an implied power to fulfill the great purpose of national defence or to raise money to prosecute a war, are a mere waste of words, as the most powerful and comprehensive means to accomplish the purpose for which the appeal is made are found in the express powers vested in Congress to lay and collect taxes, duties, imposts, and excises without limitation as to amount, to borrow money also without limitation, and to coin money, dispose of the public lands, and to appropriate all moneys in the public treasury to that purpose.

Weighed in the light of these suggestions, as the questions under discussion should be, it is plain, not only that the exercise of such an implied power is unnecessary to supply the sinews of war, but that the framers of the Constitution never intended to trust a matter of such great and vital importance as that of raising means for the national defence or for the prosecution of a war to any implication whatever, as they had learned from bitter experience that the great weakness of the Confederation during the war for independence consisted in the want of such express powers. Influenced by those considerations the framers of the Constitution not only authorized Congress to lay and collect taxes, duties, imposts and excises, to any and every extent, but also to coin money and to borrow money without any limitation as to amount, showing that the argument that to deny the implied power to make paper emissions a legal tender will be to cripple the government, is a mere chimera, without any solid constitutional foundation for its support.

Comprehensive, however, as the power of federal taxation is, being without limitation as to amount, still there are some restrictions as to the manner of its exercise, and some exceptions as to the objects to which it may be applied. Bills for raising revenue must originate in the House of Representatives; duties, imposts, and excises must be uniform throughout the United States; direct taxes must be apportioned according to numbers; regulations of commerce and revenue shall not give any preference to the ports of one State over those of another; nor shall vessels bound to or from one State be obliged to enter, clear, or pay duties in another; nor shall any tax or duty be laid on articles exported from any State.

Preparation for war may be made in peace, but neither the necessity for such preparation nor the actual existence of war can have the effect to abrogate or supersede those restrictions, or to empower Congress to tax the articles excepted from taxation by the Constitution. Implied exceptions also exist limiting the power of federal taxation as well as that of the States, and when an exception of that character is ascertained, the objects falling within it are as effectually shielded from taxation as those falling within an express exception, for the plain reason that the "government of the United States is acknowledged by all to be one of enumerated powers," from which it necessarily follows that powers not granted cannot be exercised.—McCULLOH *vs.* STATE OF MARYLAND, 4 *Wheaton*, 405.)

Moneys may be raised by taxes, duties, imposts, and excises to carry on war as well as to pay the public debt or to provide for the common defence and general welfare, but no appropriation of money to that use can be made for a period longer than two years, nor can Congress, in exercising the power to levy taxes for that purpose, or any other, abrogate or supersede those restrictions, exceptions, and limitations, as they are a part of the Constitution, and as such are as obligatory, in war as in peace, as any other rule would subvert, in time of war, every restriction, exception, limitation, and prohibition in the Constitution and invest Congress with unlimited power, even surpassing that possessed by the British Parliament.

Congress may also borrow money to carry on war, without limitation, and in exercising that express power may issue treasury notes as the requisite means for carrying the express power into execution, but Congress cannot constitute such notes a standard of value nor make them a legal-tender, neither in time of war nor in time of peace, for at least two reasons, either of which is conclusive that the exercise of such a power is not warranted by the Constitution : (1) Because the published proceedings of the convention which adopted the Constitution, and of the state conventions which ratified it, show that those who participated in those deliberations never intended to confer any such power. (2) Because such a power, if admitted to exist, would nullify the effect and operation of the express power to coin money, regulate the value thereof and of foreign coin; as it would substitute a paper medium in the place of gold and silver coin, which in itself, as compared with coin, possesses no value, is not money, either in the constitutional or commercial sense, but only a promise to pay money, is never worth par, and often much less, even as domestic exchange, and is always fluctuating and never acknowledged either as a medium of exchange or a standard of value in any foreign market known to American commerce.

Power to issue such notes, it is conceded, exists without limitation, but the question is whether the framers of the Constitution intended that Congress, in the exercise of that power or the power to borrow money, whether in peace or war, should be empowered to constitute paper emissions, of any kind, a standard of value, and make the same a legal tender in payment of debts. Mere convenience, or even a financial necessity in a single case, cannot be the test, but the question is what did the framers of the Constitution intend at the time the instrument was adopted and ratified ?

Constitutional powers, of the kind last mentioned, that is the power to ordain a standard of value and to provide a circulating medium for a legal tender, are subject to no mutations of any kind. They are the same in peace and in war. What the grants of power meant when the Constitution was adopted and ratified they mean still, and their meaning can never be changed except as described in the fifth article providing for amendments, as the Constitution " is a law for rulers and people, equally in war and in peace, and covers with the shield of its protection all classes of men and under all circumstances."—
(*Ex-parte* MILLIGAN, 4 *Wallace*, 120.)

Delegated power ought never to be enlarged beyond the fair scope of its terms, and that rule is emphatically applicable in the construction of the Constitution. Restrictions may at times be inconvenient, or even embarrassing, but the power to remove the difficulty by amendment is vested in the people, and if they do not exercise it the presumption is that the inconvenience is a less evil than the mischief to be apprehended if the restriction should be removed and the power extended, or that the existing inconvenience is the least of the two evils ; and it should never be forgotten that the government ordained and established by the Constitution is a government "of limited and enumerated powers," and that to depart from the true import and meaning of those powers is to establish a new constitution or to do for the people what they have not chosen to do for themselves, and to usurp the functions of a legislator and desert those of an expounder of the law. Arguments drawn from impolicy or inconvenience, says Judge STORY, ought here to be of no weight, as "the only sound principle is to declare *ita lex scripta est*, to follow and to obey.—(1 *Story on Constitution*, 3d ed., sec. 426.)

For these reasons I am of the opinion tnat the judgment in each of the cases before the court should be reversed.

DISSENTING OPINION BY MR. JUSTICE FIELD.

Before the Supreme Court of the United States, December Term, 1870.

The cases of WILLIAM B. KNOX, *Plaintiff in Error, vs.* PHŒBE G. LEE *and* HUGH LEE, *her husband.* In Error to the Circuit Court of the United States for the Western District of TEXAS,

and

THOMAS H. PARKER, *Plaintiff in Error, vs.* GEORGE DAVIS. In error to the Supreme Judicial Court of the Commonwealth of MASSACHUSETTS.

Whilst I agree with the Chief Justice in the views expressed in his opinion in these cases, the great importance which I attach to the question of legal tender, induces me to present some further considerations on the subject.

Nothing has been heard from counsel in these cases, and nothing from the present majority of the court, which has created a doubt in my mind of the correctness of the judgment rendered in the case of HEPBURN *vs.* GRISWOLD, (8 *Wallace*, 603,) or of the conclusions expressed in the opinion of the majority of the court as then constituted. That judgment was reached only after repeated arguments were heard from able and eminent counsel, and after every point raised on either side had been the subject of extended deliberation.

The questions presented in that case were also involved in several other cases, and had been elaborately argued in them. It is not extravagant to say that no case has ever been decided by this court since its organization, in which the questions presented were more fully argued, or more maturely considered. It was hoped that a judgment thus reached would not be lightly disturbed. It was hoped that it had settled forever that, under a constitution ordained, among other things, " to establish justice," legislation giving to one person the right to discharge his obligations to another by nominal instead of actual fulfillment, could never be justified.

I shall not comment upon the causes which have led to a reversal of that judgment. They are patent to every one. I will simply observe that the Chief Justice and the associate justices, who constituted the majority of the court when that judgment was rendered, still adhere to their former convictions. To them the reasons for the original decision are as cogent and convincing now as they were when that decision was pronounced; and to them its justice, as applied to past contracts, is as clear to-day as it was then.

In the cases now before us the questions stated, by order of the court, for the argument of counsel, do not present with entire accuracy the questions actually argued and decided. As stated, the questions are: 1st. Is the act of Congress known as the legal-tender act constitutional as to contracts made before its passage? 2nd. Is it valid as applicable to transactions since its passage?

The act thus designated as the legal-tender act is the act of Congress of February 25th, 1862, authorizing the issue of United States notes, and providing for their redemption or funding, and for funding the floating debt of the United States (12 *Statutes*, 345); and the questions, as stated, would seem to draw into discussion the validity of the entire act; whereas, the only questions intended for argument, and actually argued and decided, relate—1st, to the validity of that provision of the act which declares that these notes shall be a legal tender in payment of debts, as applied to private debts and debts of the government contracted previous to the passage of the act; and 2d, to the validity of the provision as applied to similar contracts subsequently made. The case of PARKER *vs.* DAVIS involves the consideration of the first question; and the case of KNOX *vs.* LEE is supposed by a majority of the court to present the second question.

No question was raised as to the validity of the provisions of the act authorizing the issue of the notes, and making them receivable for dues to the United States; nor do I perceive that any objection could justly be made at this day to these provisions. The issue of the notes was a proper exercise of the power to borrow money, which is granted to Congress without limitation. The extent to which the power may be exercised depends, in all cases, upon the judgment of that body as to the necessities of the government. The power to borrow includes the power to give evidences of indebtedness and obligations of repayment. Instruments of this character are among the securities of the United States mentioned in the Constitution. These securities are sometimes in the form of certificates of indebtedness, but they may be issued in any other form, and in such form and in such amounts as will fit them for general circulation, and to that end may be made payable to bearer and transferable by delivery. The form of notes, varying in amounts to suit the convenience or ability of the lender, has been found by experience a convenient form, and the one best calculated to secure the readiest acceptance and the largest loan. It has been the practice of the government to use notes of this character in raising loans and obtaining supplies, from an early period in its history, their receipt by third parties being in all cases optional.

In June, 1812, Congress passed an act which provided for the issue of treasury notes, and authorized the Secretary of the Treasury, with the approbation of the President, "to borrow from time to time, not under par, such sums" as the President might think expedient, "on the credit of such notes."—(2 *Statutes*, 766.)

In February, 1813, Congress passed another act for the issue of treasury notes, declaring "that the amount of money borrowed or ob-

Legal Tender Cases of 1871. 83

tained by virtue of the notes" issued under its second section should be a part of the money authorized to be borrowed under a previous act of the same session.—(2 *Statutes*, 801.) There are numerous other acts of a similar character on our statute books. More than twenty, I believe, were passed previous to the legal-tender act.— (*Acts of Congress authorizing the issue of Treasury notes:* June 30, 1812, *Vol. II., page* 766; February 25, 1813, *Vol. II., page* 801; March 4, 1814, *Vol. III., page* 100; December 26, 1814, *Vol. III., page* 161; February 24, 1815, *Vol. III., page* 213; October 12, 1837, *Vol. V., page* 201; May 21, 1838, *Vol. V., page* 228; March 2, 1839, *Vol. V., page* 323; March 31, 1840, *Vol. V., page* 370; February 15, 1841, *Vol. V., page* 411; January 31, 1842, *Vol. V., page* 469; April 15, 1842, *Vol. V., page* 473; August 31, 1842, *Vol. V., page* 581; March 3, 1843, *Vol. V., page* 614; July 22, 1846, *Vol. IX., page* 39; August 6, 1846, *Vol. IX., page* 64; January 28, 1847, *Vol. IX., page* 118; December 23, 1857, *Vol. XI., page* 257; March 3, 1859, *Vol. XI., page* 430.)

In all of them the issue of the notes was authorized as a means of borrowing money, or obtaining supplies, or paying the debts of the United States, and in all of them the receipt of the notes by third parties was purely voluntary. Thus, in the first act, of June, 1812, the Secretary of the Treasury was authorized, not only to borrow on the notes, but to issue such notes as the President might think expedient " in payment of supplies or debts due by the United States to such public creditors or other persons" as might " *choose to receive such notes in payment at par.*" Similar provisions are found in all the acts except where the notes are authorized simply to take up previous loans.

The issue of the notes for supplies purchased or services rendered at the request of the United States is only giving their obligations for an indebtedness thus incurred ; and the same power which authorizes the issue of notes for money must also authorize their issue for whatever is received as an equivalent for money. The result to the United States is the same as if the money were actually received for the notes and then paid out for the supplies or services.

The notes issued under the act of Congress of February 25th, 1862, differ from the treasury notes authorized by the previous acts to which I have referred, in the fact that they do not bear interest and do not designate on their face a period at which they shall be paid, features which may affect their value in the market but do not change their essential character. There cannot be, therefore, as already stated, any just objection at this day to the issue of the notes, nor to their adaptation in form for general circulation.

Nor can there be any objection to their being made receivable for dues to the United States. Their receivability in this respect is only the application to the demands of the government, and demands against it of the just principle which is applied to the demands of individuals against each other, that cross-demands shall offset and satisfy each other to the extent of their respective amounts. No rights of third parties are in any respect affected by the application of the rule here, and the purchasing and borrowing power of the notes are greatly increased by making them thus receivable for the public dues. The objection to the act does not lie in these features; it lies in the provision which declares that the notes shall be "a legal tender in payment of all debts, public and private," so far as that provision applies to private debts, and debts owing by the United States.

In considering the validity and constitutionality of this provision, I shall, in the first place, confine myself to the provision in its application to private debts. Afterwards I shall have something to say of the provision in its application to debts owing by the government.

In the discussions upon the subject of legal tender the advocates of the measure do not agree as to the power in the Constitution to which it shall be referred;—some placing it upon the power to borrow money, some on the coining power, and some on what is termed a resulting power from the general purposes of the government;—and these discussions have been accompanied by statements as to the effect of the measure, and the consequences which must have followed had it been rejected, and which will now occur if its validity be not sustained, which rest upon no solid foundation, and are not calculated to aid the judgment in coming to a just conclusion.

In what I have to say I shall endeavor to avoid any such general and loose statements, and shall direct myself to an inquiry into the nature of these powers to which the measure is referred, and the relation of the measure to them.

Now, if Congress can, by its legislative declaration, make the notes of the United States a legal tender in payment of private debts, or that is, can make them receivable against the will of the creditor in satisfaction of debts due to him by third parties,—its power in this respect is not derived from its power to borrow money, under which the notes were issued. That power is not different in its nature or essential incidents from the power to borrow possessed by individuals, and is not to receive a larger definition. Nor is it different from the power often granted to public and private corporations. The grant, it is true, is usually accompanied in these latter cases with limitations as to the amount to be borrowed, and a designation of the objects to which the money shall be applied,—limitations which in no respect affect the nature of the power. The terms "power to borrow money" have the same meaning in all these cases, and not one meaning when used by individuals, another when granted to corporations, and still a different one when possessed by Congress. They mean only a power to contract for a loan of money upon considerations to be agreed between the parties. The amount of the loan, the time of repayment, the interest it shall bear, and the form in which the obligation shall be expressed are simply matters of arrangement between the parties. They concern no one else. It is no part or incident of a contract of this character that the rights or interests of third parties, strangers to he matter, shall be in any respect affected. The transaction is completed when the lender has parted with his money, and the borrower has given his promise of repayment at the time, and in the manner, and with the securities stipulated between them.

As an inducement to the loan, and security for its repayment, the borrower may, of course, pledge such property or revenues, and annex to his promises such rights and privileges as he may possess. His stipulations in this respect are necessarily limited to his own property, rights, and privileges, and cannot extend to those of other persons.

Now, whether a borrower—be the borrower an individual, a corporation, or the government—can annex to the bonds, notes, or other evidences of debt given for the money borrowed, any quality by which they will serve as a means of satisfying the contracts of other parties, must necessarily depend upon the question whether the borrower possesses any right to interfere with such contracts, and determine how they shall be satisfied. The right of the borrower in this respect rests upon no different foundation than the right to interfere with any other property of third parties. And if it will not be contended, as I think I may assume it will not be, that the borrower possesses any right, in order to make a loan, to interfere with the tangible and visible property of third parties, I do not perceive how it can be contended that he has any right to interfere with their property when it exists in the form of contracts. A large part of the property of every commercial people exists in that form, and the principle which excludes a stranger from meddling with another's property which is visible and tangible, equally excludes him from meddling with it when existing in the form of contracts.

That an individual or a corporation borrowing possesses no power to annex to his evidences of indebtedness any quality by which the holder will be enabled to change his contracts with third parties, strangers to the loan, is admitted; but it is contended that Congress possesses such power because, in addition to the express power to borrow money, there is a clause in the Constitution which authorizes Congress to make all laws "necessary and proper" for the execution of the powers enumerated. This clause neither augments nor diminishes the expressly designated powers. It only states in terms what Congress would equally have had the right to do without its insertion in the Constitution. It is a general principle that a power to do a particular act includes the power to adopt all the ordinary and appropriate means for its execution. "Had the Constitution," says HAMILTON, in the *Federalist*, speaking of this clause, "been silent on this head, there can be no doubt that all the particular powers requisite as a means of executing the general powers would have resulted to the government by unavoidable implication. No axiom is more clearly established in law or in reason, than that whenever the end is required the means are authorized; whenever a general power to do a thing is given, every particular power necessary for doing it is included."—(*The Federalist, No. 44.*)

The subsidiary power existing without the clause in question, its insertion in the Constitution was no doubt intended, as observed by Mr. HAMILTON, to prevent "all caviling refinements" in those who might thereafter feel a disposition to curtail and evade the legitimate authorities of the Union; and also, I may add, to indicate the true sphere and limits of the implied powers.

But though the subsidiary power would have existed without this clause, there would have been the same perpetually recurring question as now, as to what laws are necessary and proper for the execution of the expressly enumerated powers.

The particular clause in question has at different times undergone elaborate discussion in Congress, in cabinets, and in the courts. Its meaning was much debated in the first Congress upon the proposition to incorporate a national bank, and afterwards in the cabinet of WASHINGTON, when that measure was presented for his approval. Mr. JEFFERSON, then Secretary of State, and Mr. HAMILTON, then Secretary of the Treasury, differed widely in their construction of the clause, and each gave his views in an elaborate opinion. Mr. JEFFERSON held that the word "necessary" restricted the power of Congress to the use of those means, without which the grant would be nugatory, thus making necessary equivalent to indispensable.

Mr. HAMILTON favored a more liberal, and, in my judgment, a more just interpretation, and contended that the terms "necessary and proper" meant no more than that the measures adopted must have an obvious relation as a means to the end intended. "If the end," he said, "be clearly comprehended within any of the specified powers, and if the measure have an obvious relation to that end, and is not forbidden by any particular provision of the Constitution, it may safely be deemed to come within the compass of the national authority." There "is also," he added, "this further criterion which may materially assist the decision. Does the proposed measure abridge a pre-existing right of any State, or of any individual? If it does not, there is a strong presumption in favor of its constitutionality; and slighter relations to any declared object may be permitted to turn the scale." From the criterion thus indicated it would seem that the distinguished statesman was of opinion, that a measure which did interfere with a pre-existing right of a State or an individual would not be constitutional.

The interpretation given by Mr. HAMILTON was substantially followed by Chief Justice MARSHALL in "McCULLOH vs. THE STATE OF MARYLAND," when, speaking for the court, he said that if the end to be accomplished by the legislation of Congress be legitimate, and within the scope of the Constitution, "all the means which are appropriate, which are plainly adapted to that end, and which are not prohibited, but are consistent with the letter and spirit of the Constitution, are constitutional." The Chief Justice did not, it is true, in terms declare that legislation which is not thus appropriate, and plainly adapted to a lawful end, is unconstitutional, but such is the plain import of the argument advanced by him; and that conclusion must also follow from the principle that, when legislation of a particular character is specially authorized, the opposite of such legislation is inhibited.

Tested by the rule given by Mr. HAMILTON, or by the rule thus laid down by this court through Mr. Chief Justice MARSHALL, the annexing of a quality to the promises of the government for money borrowed, which will enable the holder to use them as a means of satisfying the demands of third parties, cannot be sustained as the exercise of an appropriate means of borrowing. That is only appropriate which has some relation of fitness to an end. Borrowing, as already stated, is a transaction by which, on one side, the lender parts with his money, and on the other the borrower agrees to repay it in such form and at such time as may be stipulated. Though not a necessary part of the contract of borrowing, it is usual for the borrower to offer securities for the repayment of the loan. The fitness which would render a means appropriate to this transaction thus considered must have respect to the terms which are essential to the contract, or to the securities which the borrower may furnish as an inducement to the loan. The quality of legal tender does not touch the terms of the contract of borrowing, nor does it stand as a security for the loan. A security supposes some right or interest in the thing pledged, which is subject to the disposition of the borrower.

There has been much confusion on this subject from a failure to distinguish between the adaptation of particular means to an end and the effect, or supposed effect, of those means in producing results desired by the government. The argument is stated thus : the object of borrowing is to raise funds ; the annexing of the quality of legal tender to the notes of the government induces parties the more readily to loan upon them ; the result desired by the government—the acquisition of funds—is thus accomplished ; therefore, the annexing of the quality of legal tender is an appropriate means to the execution of the power to borrow. But it is evident that the same reasoning would justify, as appropriate means to the execution of this power, any measures which would result in obtaining the required funds. The annexing of a provision by which the notes of the government should serve as a free ticket in the public conveyances of the country, or for ingress into places of public amusement, or which would entitle the holder to a percentage out of the revenues of private corporations, or exempt his entire property, as well as the notes themselves, from state and municipal taxation, would produce a ready acceptance of the notes. But the advocate of the most liberal construction would hardly pretend that these measures, or similar measures touching the property of third parties, would be appropriate as a means to the execution of the power to borrow. Indeed, there is no invasion by government of the rights of third parties which might not thus be sanctioned upon the pretence that its allowance to the holder of the notes would lead to their ready acceptance, and produce the desired loan.

The actual effect of the quality of legal tender in inducing parties to receive them was necessarily limited to the amount required by existing debtors, who did not scruple to discharge with them their pre-existing liabilities. For moneys desired from other parties, or supplies required for the use of the army or navy, the provision added nothing to the value of the notes. Their borrowing power or purchasing power depended, by a general and an universal law of currency, not upon the legal-tender clause, but upon the confidence which the parties receiving the notes had in their ultimate payment. Their exchangeable value was determined by this confidence, and every person dealing in them advanced his money and regulated his charges accordingly.

The inability of mere legislation to control this universal law of currency is strikingly illustrated by the history of the bills of credit issued by the Continental Congress during our revolutionary war. From June, 1775, to March, 1780, these bills amounted to over three hundred millions. Depreciation followed as a natural consequence, commencing in 1777, when the issues only equaled fourteen millions. Previous to this time, in January, 1776, when the issues were only five millions, Congress had, by resolution, declared that if any person should be "so lost to all virtue and regard to his country" as to refuse to receive the bills in payment, he should, on conviction thereof by the committee of the city, county, or district, or, in case of appeal from their decision, by the assembly, convention, council, or committee of safety of the colony where he resided, be "deemed, published, and treated as an enemy of his country, and precluded from all trade or intercourse with the inhabitants" of the colonies.—(2 *Journals of Congress*, 21.)

And in January, 1777, when as yet the issues were only fourteen millions, Congress passed this remarkable resolution:

"Resolved, That all bills of credit emitted by authority of Congress ought to pass current in all payments, trade, and dealings in these States, and be deemed in value equal to the same nominal sums in Spanish milled dollars, and that whosoever shall offer, ask, or receive more in the said bills for any gold or silver coins, bullion, or any other species of money whatsoever, than the nominal sum or amount thereof in Spanish milled dollars, or more in the said bills for any lands, houses, goods, or commodities whatsoever than the same could be purchased at of the same person or persons in gold, silver, or any other species of money whatsoever, or shall offer to sell any goods or commodities for gold or silver coins or any other species of money whatsoever and refuse to sell the same for the said continental bills, every such person ought to be deemed an enemy to the liberty of these United States and to forfeit the value of the money so exchanged, or house, land, or commodity so sold or offered for sale. And it is recommended to the legislatures of the respective States to enact laws inflicting such forfeitures and other penalties on offenders as aforesaid as will prevent such pernicious practices. That it be recommended to the legislatures of the United States to pass laws to make the bills of credit issued by the Congress a lawful tender in payment of public and private debts, and a refusal thereof an extinguishment of such debts; that debts payable in sterling money be discharged with continental dollars at the rate of 4s. 6d. sterling per dollar, and that in discharge of all other debts and contracts continental dollars pass at the rate fixed by the respective States for the value of Spanish milled dollars."

The several States promptly responded to the recommendations of Congress and made the bills a legal tender for debts and the refusal to receive them an extinguishment of the debt.

Congress also issued, in September, 1779, a circular addressed to the people on the subject, in which they showed that the United States would be able to redeem the bills, and they repelled with indignation the suggestion that there could be any violation of the public faith. The "pride of America," said the address, "revolts from the idea; her citizens know for what purposes these emissions were made, and have repeatedly plighted their faith for the redemption of them; they are to be found in every man's possession, and every man is interested in their being redeemed; they must, therefore, entertain a high opinion of American credulity who supposes the people capable of believing, on due reflection, that all America will, against the faith, the honor, and the interest of all America, be ever prevailed upon to countenance, support, or permit so ruinous, so disgraceful a measure. We are convinced that the efforts and arts of our enemies will not be wanting to draw us into this humiliating and contemptible situation. Impelled by malice and the suggestions of chagrin and disappointment at not being able to bend our necks to the yoke, they will endeavor to force or seduce us to commit this unpardonable sin in order to subject us to the punishment due to it, and that we may thenceforth be a reproach and a by-word among the nations. Apprised of these consequences, knowing the value of national character, and impressed with a due sense of the immutable laws of justice and honor, it is impossible that America should think without horror of such an execrable deed."—(5 *Journals of Congress*, p. 351. *This address was written by Mr. Jay See Flanders' Lives and Times of the Chief Justices, vol. 1, page* 256.)

Yet in spite of the noble sentiments contained in this address, which bears the honored name of John Jay, then President of Congress and afterwards the first Chief Justice of this court, and in spite of legal-tender provisions and harsh penal statutes, the universal law of currency prevailed. Depreciation followed until it became so great that the very idea of redemption at par was abandoned.

Congress then proposed to take up the bills by issuing new bills on the credit of the several States, guaranteed by the United States, not exceeding one-twentieth of the amount of the old issue, the new bills to draw interest and be redeemable in six years. But the scheme failed and the bills became, during 1780, of so little value that they ceased to circulate and "quietly died," says the historian of the period, "in the hands of their possessors."—(*Pitkin's History*, 2 *vol., page* 157.)

And it is within the memory of all of us that during the late rebellion the notes of the United States issued under the legal-tender act rose in value in the market as the successes of our arms gave evidence of an early termination of the war, and that they fell in value with every triumph of the Confederate forces. No legislation of Congress declaring these notes to be money, instead of representatives of money or credit, could alter this result one jot or tittle. Men measured their value not by congressional declaration, which could not alter the nature of things, but by the confidence reposed in their ultimate payment.

Without the legal-tender provision the notes would have circulated equally well and answered all the purposes of government—the only direct benefit resulting from that provision arising, as already stated, from the ability it conferred upon unscrupulous debtors to discharge with them previous obligations. The notes of State banks circulated without possessing that quality and supplied a currency for the people just so long as confidence in the ability of the banks to redeem the notes continued. The notes issued by the national bank associations during the war, under the authority of Congress, amounting to three hundred millions, which were never made a legal tender, circulated equally well with the notes of the United States. Neither their utility nor their circulation was diminished in any degree by the absence of a legal-tender quality. They rose and fell in the market under the same influences and precisely to the same extent as the notes of the United States, which possessed this quality.

It is foreign, however, to my argument to discuss the utility of the legal-tender clause. The utility of a measure is not the subject of judicial cognizance, nor, as already intimated, the test of its constitutionality. But the relation of the measure as a means to an end, authorized by the Constitution, is a subject of such cognizance, and the test of its constitutionality, when it is not prohibited by any specific provision of that instrument, and is consistent with its letter and spirit. "The degree," said Hamilton, "in which a measure is necessary can never be a test of the *legal right* to adopt it. That must be a matter of opinion, and only be a test of expediency. The relation between the means and the end, between the nature of a *means* employed toward the execution of the power and the *object* of that power, must be the criterion of unconstitutionality; not the more or less of necessity or utility."

If this were not so, if Congress could not only exercise, as it undoubtedly may, unrestricted liberty of choice among the means which are appropriate and plainly adapted to the execution of an express power, but could also judge, without its conclusions being subject to question in cases involving private rights, what means are thus appropriate and adapted, our government would be, not what it was intended to be, one of limited, but one of unlimited powers.

Of course Congress must inquire in the first instance, and determine for itself not only the expediency, but the fitness to the end intended, of every measure adopted by its legislation. But the power of this tribunal to revise these determinations in cases involving private rights has been uniformly asserted, since the formation of the Constitution to this day, by the ablest statesmen and jurists of the country.

I have thus dwelt at length upon the clause of the Constitution in vesting Congress with the power to borrow money on the credit of the United States, because it is under that power that the notes of the United States were issued, and it is upon the supposed enhanced value which the quality of legal tender gives to such notes, as the means of borrowing, that the validity and constitutionality of the provision annexing this quality are founded. It is true that, in the arguments of counsel, and in the several opinions of different state courts, to which our attention has been called, and in the dissenting opinion in HEPBURN *vs.* GRISWOLD, reference is also made to other powers possessed by Congress, particularly to declare war, to suppress insurrection, to raise and support armies, and to provide and maintain a navy; all of which were called into exercise and severely taxed at the time the legal-tender act was passed. But it is evident that the notes have no relation to these powers, or to any other powers of Congress, except as they furnish a convenient means for raising money for their execution. The existence of the war only increased the urgency of the government for funds. It did not add to its powers to raise such funds, or change, in any respect, the nature of those powers or the transactions which they authorized. If the power to engraft the quality of legal tender upon the notes existed at all with Congress, the occasion, the extent, and the purpose of its exercise were mere matters of legislative discretion; and the power may be equally exerted when a loan is made to meet the ordinary expenses of government in time of peace, as when vast sums are needed to raise armies and provide navies in time of war. The wants of the government can never be the measure of its powers.

The Constitution has specifically designated the means by which funds can be raised for the uses of the government, either in war or peace. These are taxation, borrowing, coining, and the sale of its public property. Congress is empowered to levy and collect taxes, duties, imposts, and excises to any extent which the public necessities may require. Its power to borrow is equally unlimited. It can convert any bullion it may possess into coin, and it can dispose of the public lands and other property of the United States or any part of such property. The designation of these means exhausts the powers of Congress on the subject of raising money. The designation of the means is a negation of all others; for the designation would be unnecessary and absurd if the use of any and all means were permissible without it. These means exclude a resort to forced loans, and to any compulsory interference with the property of third persons, except by regular taxation in one of the forms mentioned.

But this is not all. The power to "coin money" is, in my judgment, inconsistent with and repugnant to the existence of a power to make anything but coin a legal tender. To coin money is to mould metallic substances having intrinsic value into certain forms convenient for commerce, and to impress them with the stamp of the government indicating their value. Coins are pieces of metal, of different weight and value, thus stamped by national authority. Such is the natural import of the terms "to coin money" and "coin;" and if there were any doubt that this is their meaning in the Constitution, it would be removed by the language which immediately follows the grant of the "power to coin," authorizing Congress to regulate the value of the money thus coined, and also " of foreign coin," and by the distinction made in other clauses between coin and the obligations of the general government and of the several States.

The power of regulation conferred is the power to determine the weight and purity of the several coins struck, and their consequent relation to the monetary unit which might be established by the authority of the government—a power which can be exercised with reference to the metallic coins of foreign countries, but which is incapable of execution with reference to their obligations or securities.

Then, in the clause of the Constitution immediately following, authorizing Congress " to provide for the punishment of counterfeiting the securities and current coin of the United States," a distinction between the obligations and coins of the general government is clearly made. And in the tenth section, which forbids the states to " coin money, emit bills of credit, and make anything but gold and silver coin a tender in payment of debts," a like distinction is made between coin and the obligation of the several States. The terms gold and silver as applied to the coin exclude the possibility of any other conclusion.

Now, money in the true sense of the term is not only a medium of exchange, but it is a standard of value by which all other values are measured. BLACKSTONE says, and STORY repeats his language, " money is an universal medium or common standard, by a comparison with which the value of all merchandise may be ascertained, or it is a sign which represents the respective values of all commodities." (1 *Blackstone's Commentaries*, 276 ; 1 *Story on the Constitution*, §1118.) Money being such standard, its coins or pieces are necessarily a legal tender to the amount of their respective values for all contracts or judgments payable in money, without any legislative enactment to make them so. The provisions in the different coinage acts that the coins to be struck shall be such legal tender, are merely declaratory of their effect when offered in payment, and are not essential to give them that character.

The power to coin money is, therefore, a power to fabricate coins out of metal as money, and thus make them a legal tender for their declared values as indicated by their stamp. If this be the true import and meaning of the language used, it is difficult to see how Congress can make the paper of the government a legal tender. When the Constitution says that Congress shall have the power to make metallic coins a legal tender it declares in effect that it shall make nothing else such tender. The affirmative grant is here a negative of all other power over the subject.

Besides this, there cannot well be two different standards of value, and consequently two kinds of legal tender for the discharge of obligations arising from the same transactions. The standard or tender of the lower actual value would in such case inevitably exclude and supersede the other, for no one would use the standard or tender of higher value when his purpose could be equally well accomplished by the use of the other. A practical illustration of the truth of this principle we have all seen in the effect upon coin of the act of Congress making the notes of the United States a legal tender. It drove coin from general circulation, and made it, like bullion, the subject of sale and barter in the market.

The inhibition upon the States to coin money and yet to make anything but gold and silver coin a tender in payment of debts, must be read in connection with the grant of the coinage power to Congress. The two provisions taken together indicate beyond question that the coins which the national government was to fabricate, and the foreign coins, the valuation of which it was to regulate, were to consist principally, if not entirely, of gold and silver.

The framers of the Constitution were considering the subject of money to be used throughout the entire Union when these provisions were inserted, and it is plain that they intended by them that metallic coins fabricated by the national government, or adopted from abroad by its authority, composed of the precious metals, should everywhere be the standard and the only standard of value by which exchanges could be regulated and payments made.

At that time gold and silver moulded into forms convenient for use, and stamped with their value by public authority, constituted, with the exception of pieces of copper for small values, the money of the entire civilized world. Indeed these metals divided up and thus stamped always have constituted money with all people having any civilization, from the earliest periods in the history of the world down to the present time. It was with "four hundred shekels of silver, current money with the merchant," that ABRAHAM bought the field of Machpelah, nearly four thousand years ago.—(23 *Genesis*, 16.) This adoption of the precious metals as the subject of coinage,—the material of money by all peoples in all ages of the world,—has not been the result of any vagaries of fancy, but is attributable to the fact that they of all metals alone possess the properties which are essential to a circulating medium of uniform value.

"The circulating medium of a commercial community," says Mr. WEBSTER, "must be that which is also the circulating medium of other commercial communities, or must be capable of being converted into that medium without loss. It must also be able not only to pass in payments and receipts among individuals of the same society and nation, but to adjust and discharge the balance of exchanges between different nations. It must be something which has a value abroad as well as at home, by which foreign as well as domestic debts can be satisfied. The precious metals alone answer these purposes. They alone, therefore, are money, and whatever else is to perform the functions of money must be their representative and capable of being turned into them at will. So long as bank paper retains this quality it is a substitute for money. Divested of this nothing can give it that character."—(*Webster's Works*, vol. 3, *page* 41.)

The statesmen who framed the Constitution understood this principle as well as it is understood in our day. They had seen in the experience of the revolutionary period the demoralizing tendency, the cruel injustice and the intolerable oppression of a paper currency not convertible on demand into money, and forced into circulation by legal-tender provisions and penal enactments. When they therefore were constructing a government for a country, which they could not fail to see was destined to be a mighty empire, and have commercial relations with all nations ; a government which they believed was to endure for ages, they determined to recognize in the fundamental law as the standard of value, that which ever has been and always must be recognized by the world as the true standard, and thus facilitate commerce, protect industry, establish justice, and prevent the possibility of a recurrence of the evils which they had experienced and the perpetration of the injustice which they had witnessed. "We all know," says Mr. WEBSTER, "that the establishment of a sound and uniform currency was one of the greatest ends contemplated in the adoption of the present Constitution. If we could now fully explore all the motives of those who framed, and those who supported that Constitution, perhaps we should hardly find a more powerful one than this."—(*Webster's Works, Vol. 3, p. 395.*)

And how the framers of the Constitution endeavored to establish this "sound and uniform currency" we have already seen in the clauses which they adopted providing for a currency of gold and silver coins. Their determination to sanction only a metallic currency is further evident from the debates in the convention upon the proposition to authorize Congress to emit bills on the credit of the United States. By bills of credit, as the terms were then understood, were meant paper issues, intending to circulate through the community for its ordinary purposes as money, bearing upon their face the promise of the government to pay the sums specified thereon at a future day. The original draft contained a clause giving to Congress power "to borrow money and emit bills on the credit of the United States," and when the clause came up for consideration, Mr. MORRIS moved to strike out the words "and emit bills on the credit of the United States," observing that "if the United States had credit such bills would be unnecessary ; if they had not, unjust and useless." Mr. MADISON inquired whether it would not be "sufficient to prohibit the making them a legal tender." "This will remove," he said, "the temptation to emit them with unjust views, and promissory notes in that shape may in some emergencies be best." Mr. MORRIS replied that striking out the words would still leave room for "notes of a responsible minister," which would do "all the good without the mischief." Mr. GORHAM was for striking out the words without inserting any prohibition. If the words stood, he said, they might "suggest and lead to the measure," and that the power, so far as it was necessary or safe, was "involved in that of borrowing." Mr. MASON said he was unwilling "to tie the hands of Congress," and thought Congress "would not have the power unless it were expressed." Mr. ELLSWORTH thought it "a favorable moment to shut and bar the door against paper money." "The mischiefs," he said, " of the various experiments which had been made were now fresh in the public mind, and had excited the disgust of all the respectable part of America. By withholding the power from the new government, more friends of influence would be gained to it than by almost anything else. Paper money can in no case be necessary. Give the government credit, and other resources will offer. The power may do harm, never good." Mr. WILSON thought that " it would have a most salutary influence on the credit of the United States to remove the possibility of paper money." "This expedient," he said, " can never succeed whilst its mischiefs are remembered, and as long as it can be resorted to it will be a bar to other resources." Mr. BUTLER was urgent for disarming the government of such a power, and remarked " that paper was a legal tender in no country in Europe." Mr. MASON replied that if there was no example in Europe there was none in which the government was restrained on this head, and he was averse " to tying up the hands of the legislature altogether." Mr. LANGDON preferred to reject the whole plan than retain the words.

Of those who participated in the debates only one, Mr. MERCER, expressed an opinion favorable to paper money, and none suggested that if Congress were allowed to issue the bills their acceptance should be compulsory—that is, that they should be made a legal tender. But the words were stricken out by a vote of nine states to two. Virginia voted for the motion, and Mr. MADISON has appended a note to the debates, stating that her vote was occasioned by his acquiescence, and that he " became satisfied that striking out the words would not disable the government from the use of public notes, as far as they could be safe and proper; and would only cut off the pretext for a *paper currency*, and particularly for making the bills *a tender* either for public or private debts."—(*Madison's Papers*, vol. 3, p. 1346.

If anything is manifest from these debates it is that the members of the convention intended to withhold from Congress the power to issue bills to circulate as money,—that is, to be receivable in compulsory payment, or in other words having the quality of legal tender,— and that the express power to issue the bills was denied, under an apprehension that if granted it would give a pretext to Congress, under the idea of declaring their effect, to annex to them that quality. The issue of notes simply as a means of borrowing money, which of course would leave them to be received at the option of parties, does not appear to have been seriously questioned. The circulation of notes thus issued as a voluntary currency and their receipt in that character in payment of taxes, duties, and other public expenses, was not subject to the objections urged.

I am aware of the rule that the opinions and intentions of individual members of the convention, as expressed in its debates and proceedings, are not to control the construction of the plain language of the Constitution or narrow down the powers which that instrument confers. Members, it is said, who did not participate in the debate may have entertained different views from those expressed. The several State conventions to which the Constitution was submitted may have differed widely from each other and from its framers in their interpretation of its clauses. We all know that opposite opinions on many points were expressed in the conventions, and conflicting reasons were urged both for the adoption and the rejection of that instrument. All this is very true, but it does not apply in the present case, for on the subject now under consideration there was everywhere, in the several State conventions and in the discussions before the people, an entire uniformity of opinion, so far as we have any record of its expression, and that concurred with the intention of the convention, as disclosed by its debates, that the Constitution withheld from Congress all power to issue bills to circulate as money, meaning by that bills made receivable in compulsory payment, or, in other words, having the quality of legal tender. Every one appears to have understood that the power of making paper issues a legal tender, by Congress or by the States, was absolutely and forever prohibited.

Mr. LUTHER MARTIN, a member of the convention, in his speech before the MARYLAND legislature, as reported in his letter to that body, states the arguments urged against depriving Congress of the power to emit bills of credit, and then says that a "majority of the convention, being wise beyond every event and being willing to risk any political evil rather than admit the idea of a paper emission in any possible case, refused to trust this authority to a government to which they were lavishing the most unlimited powers of taxation and to the mercy of which they were willing blindly to trust the liberty and property of the citizens of every State in the Union, *and they erased that clause from the system.*"

Not only was this construction given to the Constitution by its framers and the people in their discussions at the time it was pending before them, but until the passage of the act of 1862, a period of nearly three-quarters of a century, the soundness of this construction was never called in question by any legislation of Congress or the opinion of any judicial tribunal. Numerous acts, as already stated, were passed during this period, authorizing the issue of notes for the purpose of raising funds or obtaining supplies, but in none of them was the acceptance of the notes made compulsory. Only one instance have I been able to find in the history of congressional proceedings where it was even suggested that it was within the competency of Congress to annex to the notes the quality of legal tender, and this occurred in 1814. The government was then greatly embarrassed from the want of funds to continue the war existing with Great Britain, and a member from Georgia introduced into the House of Representatives several resolutions directing an inquiry into the expediency of authorizing the treasury to issue notes convenient for circulation and making provision for the purchase of supplies in each State. Among the resolutions was one declaring that the notes to be issued should be a legal tender for debts due or subsequently becoming due between citizens of the United States and between citizens and foreigners. The House agreed to consider all the resolutions but the one containing the legal-tender provision. That it refused to consider by a vote of more than two to one.—(*Benton's Abridgment*, vol. 5, p. 361.)

As until the act of 1862 there was no legislation making the acceptance of notes issued on the credit of the United States compulsory, the construction of the clause of the Constitution, containing the grant of the coinage power never came directly before this court for construction, and the attention of the court was only incidentally drawn to it. But whenever the court spoke on the subject, even incidentally, its voice was in entire harmony with that of the convention.

Thus, in GWIN *vs.* BREEDLOVE (2 *Howard*, 38), where a marshal of Mississippi, commanded to collect a certain amount of dollars on execution, received the amount in bank notes, it was held that he was liable to the plaintiff in gold and silver. " By the Constitution of the United States," said the court, " gold or silver coin made current by law can only be tendered in payment of debts."

And in the case of the UNITED STATES *vs.* MARIGOLD (9 *Howard*, 567), where the question arose whether Congress had power to enact certain provisions of law for the punishment of persons bringing into the United States counterfeit coin with intent to pass it, the court said: These provisions " appertain to the execution of an important trust invested by the Constitution, and to the obligation to fulfill that trust on the part of the government, namely, the trust and the duty of creating and maintaining a uniform and pure metallic standard of value throughout the Union. The power of coining money and of regulating its value was delegated to Congress by the Constitution for the very purpose, as assigned by the framers of that instrument, of creating and preserving the uniformity and purity of such a standard of value, and on account of the impossibility which was foreseen of otherwise preventing the inequalities and the confusion necessarily incident to different views of policy, which in different communities would be brought to bear on this subject. The power to coin money being thus given to Congress, founded on public necessity, it must carry with it the correlative power of protecting the creature and object of that power."

It is difficult to perceive how the trust and duty here designated, of " creating and maintaining a uniform and metallic standard of value throughout the Union," is discharged, when another standard of lower value and fluctuating character is authorized by law, which necessarily operates to drive the first from circulation.

In addition to all the weight of opinion I have mentioned we have, to the same purport, from the adoption of the Constitution up to the passage of the act of 1862, the united testimony of the leading statesmen and jurists of the country. Of all the men who, during that period, participated with any distinction in the councils of the nation, not one can be named who ever asserted any different power in Congress than what I have mentioned. As observed by the Chief Justice, statesmen who disagreed widely on other points agreed on this.

Mr WEBSTER, who has always been regarded by a large portion of his countrymen as one of the ablest and most enlightened expounders of the Constitution, did not seem to think there was any doubt on the subject, although he belonged to the class who advocated the largest exercise of powers by the general government. From his first entrance into public life, in 1812, he gave great consideration to the subject of the currency, and in an elaborate speech in the Senate, in 1836, he said: "Currency, in a large and perhaps just sense, includes not only gold and silver and bank bills, but bills of exchange also. It may include all that adjusts exchanges and settles balances in the operations of trade and business; but if we understand by currency the legal money of the country, and that which constitutes a lawful tender for debts, and is the statute measure of value, then undoubtedly nothing is included but gold and silver. Most unquestionably there is no legal tender, and there can be no legal tender in this country, under the authority of this government or any other, but gold and silver,—either the coinage of our own mints or foreign coins, at rates regulated by Congress. This is a constitutional principle perfectly plain, and of the very highest importance. The states are expressly prohibited from making anything but gold and silver a tender in payment of debts, and, although no such express prohibition is applied to Congress, yet, as Congress has no power granted to it in this respect but to coin money, and to regulate the value of foreign coins, it clearly has no power to substitute paper, or anything else, for coin as a tender in payment of debts and in discharge of contracts. Congress has exercised this power fully in both its branches. It has coined money, and still coins it; it has regulated the value of foreign coins, and still regulates their value. The legal tender, therefore, the constitutional standard of value, is established and cannot be overthrown. To overthrow it would shake the whole system."

If, now, we consider the history of the times when the Constitution was adopted; the intentions of the framers of that instrument, as shown in their debates; the contemporaneous exposition of the coinage power in the State conventions assembled to consider the Constitution, and in the public discussions before the people; the natural meaning of the terms used; the nature of the Constitution itself as creating a government of enumerated powers; the legislative exposition of nearly three-quarters of a century; the opinions of judicial tribunals, and the recorded utterances of statesmen, jurists, and commentators, it would seem impossible to doubt that the only standard of value authorized by the Constitution was to consist of metallic coins struck or regulated by the direction of Congress, and that the power to establish any other standard was denied by that instrument.

There are other considerations besides those I have stated, which are equally convincing against the constitutionality of the legal-tender provision of the act of February 25th, 1862, so far as it applies to private debts and debts by the government contracted previous to its passage. That provision operates directly to impair the obligation of such contracts. In the dissenting opinion, in the case of HEPBURN *vs.* GRISWOLD, this is admitted to be its operation, and the position is taken that, while the Constitution forbids the States to pass such laws, it does not forbid Congress to do this, and the power to establish a uniform system of bankruptcy, which is expressly conferred, is mentioned in support of the position. In some of the opinions of the state courts, to which our attention has been directed, it is denied that the provision in question impairs the obligation of previous contracts, it being asserted that a contract to pay money is satisfied, according to its meaning, by the payment of that which is money when the payment is made, and that if the law does not interfere with this mode of satisfaction, it does not impair the obligation of the contract. This position is true so long as the term money represents the same thing in both cases or their actual equivalents, but it is not true when the term has different meanings. Money is a generic term, and contracts for money are not made without a specification of the coins or denominations of money, and the number of them intended, as eagles, dollars, or cents; and it will not be pretended that a contract for a specified number of eagles can be satisfied by a delivery of an equal number of dollars, although both eagles and dollars are money; nor would it thus be contended, though at the time the contract matured the legislature had determined to call dollars eagles. Contracts are made for things, not names or sounds, and the obligation of a contract arises from its terms and the means which the law affords for its enforcement.

A law which changes the terms of the contract, either in the time or mode of performance, or imposes new conditions, or dispenses with those expressed, or authorizes for its satisfaction something different from that provided, is a law which impairs its obligation, for such a law relieves the parties from the moral duty of performing the original stipulations of the contract, and it prevents their legal enforcement.

The notion that contracts for the payment of money stand upon any different footing in this respect from other contracts appears to have had its origin in certain old English cases, particularly that of mixed money (*Davies' Reports*, 48), which were decided upon the force of the prerogative of the king with respect to coin, and have no weight as applied to powers possessed by Congress under our Constitution. The language of Mr. Chief Justice MARSHALL in FAW *vs.* MARSTELLER, 2 *Cranch*, 20, which is cited in support of this notion can only be made to express concurrence with it, when detached from its context and read separated from the facts, in reference to which it was used.

It is obvious that the act of 1862, changes the terms of contracts for the payment of money made previous to its passage, in every essential particular. All such contracts had reference to metallic coins, struck or regulated by Congress, and composed principally of gold and silver, which constituted the legal money of the country. The several coinage acts had fixed the weight, purity, forms, impressions and denominations of these coins, and had provided that their value should be certified by the form and impress which they received at the mint.

They had established the dollar as the money unit, and prescribed the grains of silver it should contain, and the grains of gold which should compose the different gold coins. Every dollar was therefore a piece of gold or silver certified to be of a specified weight and purity, by its form and impress. A contract to pay a specified number of dollars was then a contract to deliver the designated number of pieces of gold or silver of this character; and by the laws of Congress and of the several States the delivery of such dollars could be enforced by the holder.

The act of 1862 changes all this; it declares that gold or silver dollars need not be delivered to the creditor according to the stipulations of the contract; that they need not be delivered at all; that promises of the United States, with which the creditor has had no relations, to pay these dollars, at some uncertain future day, shall be received in discharge of the contracts;—in other words that the holder of such contracts shall take in substitution for them different contracts with another party, less valuable to him, and surrender the original.

Taking it, therefore, for granted that the law plainly impairs the obligation of such contracts, I proceed to inquire whether it is for that reason subject to any constitutional objection. In the dissenting opinion in HEPBURN vs. GRISWOLD, it is said, as already mentioned, that the Constitution does not forbid legislation impairing the obligation of contracts.

It is true there is no provision in the Constitution forbidding in express terms such legislation. And it is also true that there are express powers delegated to Congress, the execution of which necessarily operates to impair the obligation of contracts. It was the object of the framers of that instrument to create a national government competent to represent the entire country in its relations with foreign nations and to accomplish by its legislation measures of common interest to all the people, which the several States in their independent capacities were incapable of effecting, or if capable, the execution of which would be attended with great difficulty and embarrassment. They, therefore, clothed Congress with all the powers essential to the successful accomplishment of these ends, and carefully withheld the grant of all other powers. Some of the powers granted, from their very nature, interfere in their execution with contracts of parties. Thus war suspends intercourse and commerce between citizens or subjects of belligerent nations; it renders during its continuance the performance of contracts previously made, unlawful. These incidental consequences were contemplated in the grant of the war power. So the regulation of commerce and the imposition of duties may so affect the prices of articles imported or manufactured as to essentially alter the value of previous contracts respecting them; but this incidental consequence was seen in the grant of the power over commerce and duties. There can be no valid objection to laws passed in execution of express powers that consequences like these follow incidentally from their execution. But it is otherwise when such consequences do not follow incidentally, but are directly enacted.

The only express authority for any legislation affecting the obligation of contracts is found in the power to establish a uniform system of bankruptcy, the direct object of which is to release insolvent debtors from their contracts upon the surrender of their property. From this express grant in the Constitution I draw a very different conclusion from that drawn in the dissenting opinion in HEPBURN *vs.* GRISWOLD, and in the opinion of the majority of the court just delivered. To my mind it is a strong argument that there is no general power in Congress to interfere with contracts, that a special grant was regarded as essential to authorize an uniform system of bankruptcy. If such general power existed the delegation of an express power in the case of bankrupts was unnecessary. As very justly observed by counsel, if this sovereign power could be taken in any case without express grant, it could be taken in connection with bankruptcies, which might be regarded in some respects as a regulation of commerce made in the interest of traders.

The grant of a limited power over the subject of contracts necessarily implies that the framers of the Constitution did not intend that Congress should exercise unlimited power, or any power less restricted. The limitation designated is the measure of Congressional power over the subject. This follows from the nature of the instrument, as one of enumerated powers.

The doctrine that where a power is not expressly forbidden it may be exercised, would change the whole character of our government. As I read the writings of the great commentators and the decisions of this court, the true doctrine is the exact reverse, that if a power is not in terms granted, and is not necessary and proper for the exercise of a power thus granted, it does not exist.

The position that Congress possesses some undefined power to do anything which it may deem expedient, as a resulting power from the general purposes of the government, which is advanced in the opinion of the majority, would of course settle the question under consideration without difficulty, for it would end all controversy by changing our government from one of enumerated powers to one resting in the unrestrained will of Congress.

"The government of the United States," says Mr. Chief Justice MARSHALL, speaking for the court in MARTIN *vs.* HUNTER'S LESSEE, (1 *Wheaton*, 326,) "can claim no powers which are not granted to it by the Constitution, and the powers actually granted must be such as are expressly given or given by necessary implication." This implication, it is true, may follow from the grant of several express powers as well as from one alone, but the power implied must, in all cases, be subsidiary to the execution of the powers expressed. The language of the Constitution respecting the writ of habeas corpus, declaring that it shall not be suspended unless, when, in cases of rebellion or invasion, the public safety may require it, is cited as showing that the power to suspend such writ exists somewhere in the Constitution; and the adoption of the amendments is mentioned as evidence that important powers were understood by the people who adopted the Constitution to have been created by it, which are not enumerated, and are not included incidentally in any of those enumerated.

The answer to this position is found in the nature of the Constitution, as one of granted powers, as stated by Mr. Chief Justice MARSHALL. The inhibition upon the exercise of a specified power does not warrant the implication that, but for such inhibition, the power might have been exercised. In the convention which framed the Constitution a proposition to appoint a committee to prepare a bill of rights was unanimously rejected upon the ground that such a bill would contain various exceptions to powers not granted, and on this very account would afford a pretext for asserting more than was granted.— (*Lloyd's Debates*, 433, 437.) In the discussions before the people, when the adoption of the Constitution was pending, no objection was urged with greater effect than this absence of a bill of rights, and in one of the numbers of the Federalist, Mr. HAMILTON endeavored to combat the objection. After stating several reasons why such a bill was not necessary, he said : " I go further and affirm that bills of rights, in the sense and to the extent they are contended for, are not only unnecessary in the proposed Constitution, but would even be dangerous. They would contain various exceptions to powers not granted, and on this very account would afford a colorable pretext to claim more than were granted. For why declare that things shall not be done which there is no power to do ? Why, for instance, should it be said that the liberty of the press shall not be restrained when no power is given by which restrictions may be imposed ? I will not contend that such a provision would confer a regulating power, but it is evident that it would furnish to men disposed to usurp a plausible pretence for claiming that power. They might urge, with a semblance of reason, that the Constitution ought not to be charged with the absurdity of providing against the abuse of an authority which was not given, and that the provision against restraining the liberty of the press afforded a clear implication that a right to prescribe proper regulations concerning it was intended to be vested in the national government. This may serve as a specimen of the numerous handles which would be given to the doctrine of constructive powers by the indulgence of an injudicious zeal for bills of rights."— (*The Federalist, No.* 84.)

When the amendments were presented to the States, for adoption, they were preceded by a preamble stating that the conventions of a number of the States had, at the time of their adopting the Constitution, expressed a desire, " in order to prevent *misconception or abuse* of its powers, that further declaratory and restrictive clauses should be added."

Now, will any one pretend that Congress could have made a law respecting an establishment of religion, or prohibiting the free exercise thereof, or abridging the freedom of speech, or the right of the people to assemble and petition the government for a redress of grievances, had not prohibitions upon the exercise of any such legislative power been embodied in an amendment ?

How truly did HAMILTON say that, had a bill of rights been inserted in the Constitution, it would have given a handle to the doctrine of constructive powers. We have this day an illustration, in the opinion of the majority, of the very claim of constructive power which he apprehended, and it is the first instance, I believe, in the history of this court, when the possession by Congress of such constructive power has been asserted.

The interference with contracts, by the legislation of the several States previous to the adoption of the Constitution, was the cause of great oppression and injustice. "Not only," says STORY, "was paper money issued and declared to be a tender in payment of debts, but laws of another character, well known under the appellation of tender laws, appraisement laws, instalment laws, and suspension laws, were from time to time enacted, which prostrated all private credit and all private morals. By some of these laws the due payment of debts was suspended; debts were, in violation of the very terms of the contract, authorized to be paid by instalments at different periods; property of any sort, however worthless, either real or personal, might be tendered by the debtor in payment of his debts, and the creditor was compelled to take the property of the debtor, which he might seize on execution, at an appraisement wholly disproportionate to its known value. Such grievances and oppressions and others of a like nature were the ordinary results of legislation during the revolutionary war and the intermediate period down to the formation of the Constitution. They entailed the most enormous evils on the country and introduced a system of fraud, chicanery, and profligacy, which destroyed all private confidence and all industry and enterprise."—(*Story's Com., sec.* 1371.)

To prevent the recurrence of evils of this character not only was the clause inserted in the Constitution prohibiting the States from issuing bills of credit and making anything but gold and silver a tender in payment of debts, but also the more general prohibition from passing any law impairing the obligation of contracts. "To restore public confidence completely," says Chief Justice MARSHALL, "it was necessary not only to prohibit the use of particular means by which it might be effected, but to prohibit the use of any means by which the same mischief might be produced. The convention appears to have intended to establish a great principle, that contracts should be inviolable."—STURGIS *vs.* CROWNINSHIELD, 4 *Wheaton*, 206.)

It would require very clear evidence, one would suppose, to induce a belief that with the evils, resulting from what MARSHALL terms the system of lax legislation following the revolution, deeply impressed on their minds, the framers of the Constitution intended to vest in the new government, created by them, this dangerous and despotic power which they were unwilling should remain with the States, and thus widen the possible sphere of its exercise.

When the possession of this power has been asserted in argument (for until now it has never been asserted in any decision of this court) it has been in cases where a supposed public benefit resulted from the legislation, or where the interference with the obligation of the contract was very slight. Whenever a clear case of injustice, in the absence of such supposed public good, is stated, the exercise of the power by the government is not only denounced, but the existence of the power is denied. No one, indeed, is found bold enough to contend that if A has a contract for one hundred acres of land, or one hundred pounds of fruit, or one hundred yards of cloth, Congress can pass a law compelling him to accept one-half of the quantity in satisfaction of the contract. But Congress has the same power to establish a standard of weights and measures as it has to establish a standard of value, and can, from time to time, alter such standard. It can declare that the acre shall consist of eighty square rods instead of one hundred and sixty, the pound of eight ounces instead of sixteen, and the foot of six inches instead of twelve, and if it could compel the acceptance of the same *number* of acres, pounds, or yards, after such alteration instead of the actual *quantity* stipulated, then the acceptance of one-half of the quantity originally designated could be directly required without going through the form of altering the standard. No just man could be imposed upon by this use of words in a double sense, where the same names were applied to denote different quantities of the same thing, nor would his condemnation of the wrong committed in such case be withheld, because the attempt was made to conceal it by this jugglery of words.

The power of Congress to interfere with contracts for the payment of money is not greater or in any particular different from its power with respect to contracts for lands or goods. The contract is not fulfilled any more in one case than in the other by the delivery of a thing which is not stipulated, because by legislative action it is called by the same name. Words in contracts are to be construed in both cases in the sense in which they were understood by the parties at the time of the contract.

Let us for a moment see where the doctrine of the power asserted will lead. Congress has the undoubted right to give such denominations as it chooses to the coins struck by its authority, and to change them. It can declare that the dime shall hereafter be called a dollar, or, what is the same thing, it may declare that the dollar shall hereafter be composed of the grains of silver which now compose the dime. But would any body pretend that a contract for dollars, composed as at present, could be satisfied by the delivery of an equal number of dollars of the new issue? I have never met any one who would go to that extent. The answer always has been, that would be too flagrantly unjust to be tolerated. Yet enforcing the acceptance of paper promises or paper dollars, if the promises can be so called, in place of gold or silver dollars, is equally enforcing a departure from the terms of the contract, the injustice of the measure depending entirely upon the actual value in the time of the promises in the market. Now reverse the case. Suppose Congress should declare that hereafter the eagle should be called a dollar or that the dollar should be composed of as many grains of gold as the eagle, would any body for a moment contend that a contract for dollars, composed as now of silver, should be satisfied by dollars composed of gold? I am confident that no judge sitting on this bench, and, indeed, that no judge in Christendom, could be found who would sanction the monstrous wrong by decreeing that the debtor could only satisfy his contract in such case by paying ten times the value originally stipnlated. The natural sense of right which is implanted in every mind would revolt from such supreme injustice. Yet there cannot be one law for debtors and another law for creditors. If the contract can at one time be changed by congressional legislation for the benefit of the debtor it may at another time be changed for the benefit of the creditor.

For acts of flagrant injustice such as those mentioned there is no authority in any legislative body, even though not restrained by any express constitutional prohibition. For as there are unchangeable principles of right and morality, without which society would be impossible, and men would be but wild beasts preying upon each other, so there are fundamental principles of eternal justice, upon the existence of which all constitutional government is founded, and without which government would be an intolerable and hateful tyranny. There are acts, says Mr. Justice CHASE, in CALDER vs. BULL, (3 *Dallas*, 388,) which the federal and State legislatures cannot do, without exceeding their authority. Among these he mentions a law which punishes a citizen for an innocent action; a law that destroys or impairs the lawful private contracts of citizens; a law that makes a man a judge in his own cause; and a law that takes the property from A and gives it to B. "It is against all reason and right," says the learned justice, " for a people to entrust a legislature with such powers; and therefore it cannot be presumed that they have done it. The genius, the nature, and the spirit of our State governments amount to a prohibition of such acts of legislation, and the general principles of law and reason forbid them. The legislature may enjoin, permit, forbid, and punish; they may declare new crimes, and establish rules of conduct for all its citizens in future cases; they may command what is right and prohibit what is wrong, but they cannot change innocence into guilt, or punish innocence as a crime, or violate the rights of an antecedent lawful private contract, or the right of private property. To maintain that our federal or State legislature possess such powers, if they had not been expressly restrained, would, in my opinion, be a political heresy, altogether inadmissible in our free republican government."

In OGDEN vs. SAUNDERS, (12 *Wheaton*, 303,) Mr. Justice THOMPSON, referring to the provisions in the Constitution forbidding the States to pass any bill of attainder, ex post facto law, or law impairing the obligation of contracts, says : "Neither provision can strictly be considered as introducing any new principle, but only for greater security and safety to incorporate into this charter provisions admitted by all to be among the first principles of government. No State court would, I presume, sanction and enforce an ex post facto law if no such prohibition was contained in the Constitution of the United States; so, neither would retrospective laws, taking away vested rights, be enforced. Such laws are repugnant to those fundamental principles upon which every just system of laws is founded. It is an elementary principle, adopted and sanctioned by the courts of justice in this country and in Great Britain, whenever such laws have come under consideration, and yet retrospective laws are clearly within this prohibition."

In WILKESON vs. LELAND, (2 Peters, 657,) Mr. Justice STORY, whilst commenting upon the power of the legislature of Rhode Island under the charter of CHARLES II., said : " The fundamental maxims of a free government seem to require that the rights of personal liberty and private property should be held sacred. At least no court of justice in this country would be warranted in assuming that the power to violate and disregard them, a power so repugnant to the common principles of justice and civil liberty, lurked under any general grant of legislative authority, or ought to be implied from any general expressions of the will of the people. The people ought not to be presumed to part with rights so vital to their security and wellbeing without very strong and direct expressions of such an intention."

Similar views to those cited from the opinions of CHASE, THOMPSON, STORY, and MARSHALL, are found scattered through the opinions of the judges who have preceded us on this bench. As against their collective force the remark of Mr. Justice WASHINGTON, in the case of EVANS vs. EATON, is without significance.—(1 Peters, Cir. Ct., 323.) That was made at *nisi prius* in answer to a motion for a nonsuit, in an action brought for an infringement of a patent right. The State of Pennsylvania had, in March, 1787, which was previous to the adoption of the Constitution, given to the plaintiff the exclusive right to make, use, and vend his invention for fourteen years. In January, 1808, the United States issued to him a patent for the invention for fourteen years from that date. It was contended, for the non-suit, that after the expiration of the plaintiff's privilege granted by the State, the right to his invention became invested in the people of the State, by an implied contract with the government, and, therefore, that Congress could not consistently with the Constitution grant to the plaintiff an exclusive right to the invention. The court replied that neither the premises upon which the motion was founded, nor the conclusion, could be admitted ; that it was not true that the grant of an exclusive privilege to an invention for a limited time implied a binding and irrevocable contract with the people that at the expiration of the period limited the invention should become their property ; and that even if the premises were true, there was nothing in the Constitution which forbade Congress to pass laws violating the obligation of contracts.

The motion did not merit any consideration, as the federal court had no power to grant a non-suit against the will of the plaintiff in any case. The expression under these circumstances of any reason why the court would not grant the motion, if it possessed the power, was aside the case, and is not, therefore, entitled to any weight whatever as authority. It is true, however, as observed by the court, that no such contract with the public, as stated, was implied, and inasmuch as Congress was expressly authorized by the Constitution to secure for a limited time to inventors the exclusive right to their discoveries, it had the power in that way to impair the obligation of such a contract, if any had existed. And this is, perhaps, all that Mr. Justice WASHINGTON meant. It is evident from his language in OGDEN *vs.* SAUNDERS, that he repudiated the existence of any general power in Congress to destroy or impair vested private rights.

What I have heretofore said respecting the power of Congress to make the notes of the United States a legal tender in payment of debts contracted previous to the act of 1862, and to interfere with contracts, has had reference to debts and contracts between citizens. But the same power which is asserted over these matters is also asserted with reference to previous debts owing by the government, and must equally apply to contracts between the government and the citizen. The act of 1862 declares that the notes issued shall be a legal tender in payment of *all debts, public and private,* with the exception of duties on imports and interest on the public debt. If they are a legal tender for antecedent private debts, they are also a legal tender for such debts owing by the United States, except in the cases mentioned. That any exception was made was a mere matter of legislative discretion. Express contracts for the payment of gold or silver have been maintained by this court, and specifically enforced on the ground that, upon a proper construction of the act of 1862, in connection with other acts, Congress intended to except these contracts from the operation of the legal tender provision. But the power covers all cases if it exist at all. The power to make the notes of the United States the legal equivalent to gold and silver necessarily includes the power to cancel with them specific contracts for gold as well as money contracts generally. Before the passage of the act of 1862, there was no legal money except that which consisted of metallic coins, struck or regulated by the authority of Congress. Dollars then meant, as already said, certain pieces of gold or silver, certified to be of a prescribed weight and purity by their form and impress received at the mint. The designation of dollars, in previous contracts, meant gold or silver dollars as plainly as if those metals were specifically named.

It follows, then, logically, from the doctrine advanced by the majority of the court as to the power of Congress over the subject of legal tender, that Congress may borrow gold coin upon a pledge of the public faith to repay gold at the maturity of its obligations, and yet, in direct disregard of its pledge, in open violation of faith, may compel the lender to take, in place of the gold stipulated, its own promises; and that legislation of this character would not be in violation of the Constitution, but in harmony with its letter and spirit.

The government is, at the present time, seeking, in the market of the world, a loan of several hundred millions of dollars in gold, upon securities containing the promises of the United States to repay the money, principal and interest, in gold; yet this court, the highest tribunal of the country, this day declares, by its solemn decision, that should such loan be obtained, it is entirely competent for Congress to pay it off, not in gold, but in notes of the United States themselves, payable at such time and in such manner as Congress may itself determine, and that legislation sanctioning such gross breach of faith would not be repugnant to the fundamental law of the land.

What is this but declaring that repudiation by the government of the United States of its solemn obligations would be constitutional? Whenever the fulfillment of the obligation in the manner stipulated is refused, and the acceptance of something different from that stipulated is enforced against the will of the creditor, a breach of faith is committed; and to the extent of the difference of value between the thing stipulated and the thing which the creditor is compelled to receive, there is repudiation of the original obligation. I am not willing to admit that the Constitution, the boast and glory of our country, would sanction or permit any such legislation. Repudiation in any form, or to any extent, would be dishonor, and for the commission of this public crime no warrant, in my judgment, can ever be found in that instrument.

Some stress has been placed in argument, in support of the asserted power of Congress over the subject of legal tender, in the fact that Congress can regulate the alloy of the coins issued under its authority, and has exercised its power in this respect, without question, by diminishing, in some instances, the actual quantity of gold or silver they contain. Congress, it is assumed, can thus put upon the coins issued other than their intrinsic value; therefore, it is argued Congress may, by its declaration, give a value to the notes of the United States, issued to be used as money, other than that which they actually possess.

The assumption and the inference are both erroneous, and the argument thus advanced is without force, and is only significant of the weakness of the position which has to rest for its support on an assumed authority of the government to debase the coin of the country.

Undoubtedly Congress can alter the value of the coins issued by its authority, by increasing or diminishing, from time to time, the alloy they contain, just as it may alter, at its pleasure, the denominations of the several coins issued, but there its power stops. It cannot make these altered coins the equivalent of the coins in their previous condition; and, if the new coins should retain the same names as the original, they would only be current at their true value. Any declaration that they should have any other value would be inoperative in fact, and a monstrous disregard by Congress of its constitutional duty. The power to coin money, as already declared by this court, is a great trust devolved upon Congress, carrying with it the duty of creating and maintaining an uniform standard of value throughout the Union, (U. S. vs. MARIGOLD, 9 *How.*, 567,) and it would be a manifest abuse of this trust to give to the coins issued by its authority any other than their real value. By debasing the coins, when once the standard is fixed, is meant giving to the coins, by their form and impress, a certificate of their having a relation to that standard different from that which, in truth, they possess; in other words, giving to the coins a false certificate of their value. Arbitrary and profligate governments have often resorted to this miserable scheme of robbery, which MILL designates as a shallow and impudent artifice, the "least covert of all modes of knavery, which consists in calling a shilling a pound, that a debt of one hundred pounds may be canceled by the payment of one hundred shillings."—(*Mill's Political Economy, Vol. 2, page* 20.

In this country no such debasement has ever been attempted, and I feel confident that none will ever be tolerated. The changes in the quantity of alloy in the different coins has been made from time to time, not with any idea of debasing them, but for the purpose of preserving the proper relative value between gold and silver. The first coinage act, passed in 1792, provided that the coins should consist of gold, silver, and copper—the coins of cents and half-cents consisting of copper, and the other coins consisting of gold and silver—and that the relative value of gold and silver should be as fifteen to one, that is, that an ounce of gold should be taken as the equal in value of fifteen ounces of silver.

In progress of time, owing to the increased production of silver, particularly from the mines of Mexico and South America, this relative value was changed. Silver declined in relative value to gold until it bore the relation of one to sixteen, instead of one to fifteen. The result was that the gold was bought up as soon as coined, being worth intrinsically sixteen times the value of silver, and yet passing by law only at fifteen times such value, and was sent out of the country to be re-coined. The attention of Congress was called to this change in the relative value of the two metals and the consequent disappearance of gold coin. This led, in 1834 (4 *United States Statutes at Large, page* 699), to an act adjusting the rate of gold coin to its true relation to silver coin.

The discovery of gold in California, some years afterwards, and the great production of that metal, again changed, in another direction, the relative value of the two metals. Gold declined, or in other words, silver was at a premium, and as gold coin before 1834 was bought up, so now silver coin was bought up and a scarcity of small coin for change was felt in the community. Congress again interfered, and in 1853 reduced the amount of silver in coins representing fractional parts of a dollar, but even then these coins were restricted from being a legal tender for sums exceeding five dollars, although the small silver coins of previous issue continued to be a legal tender for any amount. Silver pieces of the denomination of three cents had been previously authorized in 1851, but were only made a tender for sums of thirty cents and under. These coins did not express their actual value, and their issue was soon stopped, and in 1853 their value was increased to the standard of coins of other fractional parts of a dollar.

The whole of this subject has been fully and satisfactorily explained in the very able and learned argument of the counsel who contended for the maintenance of the original decision of this court in HEPBURN *vs.* GRISWOLD. He showed by the debates that Congress has been moved, in all its actions under the coinage power, only by an anxious desire to ascertain the true relative value of the two precious metals, and to fix the coinage in accordance with it; and that in no case has any deviation from intrinsic value been permitted except in coins for fractional parts of a dollar, and even that has been only of so slight a character as to prevent them from being converted into bullion, the actual depreciation being made up by their portability and convenience.

It follows, from this statement of the action of Congress in altering at different times the alloy of certain coins, that the assumption of power to stamp metal with an arbitrary value and give it currency, does not rest upon any solid foundation, and that the argument built thereon goes with it to the ground.

I have thus far spoken of the legal-tender provision with particular reference to its application to debts contracted previous to its passage. It only remains to say a few words as to its validity when applied to subsequent transactions.

So far as subsequent contracts are made payable in notes of the United States, there can of course be no objection to their specific enforcement by compelling a delivery of an equal amount of the notes, or by a judgment in damages for their value as estimated in gold or silver dollars; nor would there be any objection to such enforcement if the legal-tender provision had never existed. From the general use of the notes throughout the country and the disappearance of gold and silver coin from circulation, it may perhaps be inferred, in most cases, that notes of the United States are intended by the parties where gold or silver dollars are not expressly designated, except in contracts made in the Pacific States, where the constitutional currency has always continued in use. As to subsequent contracts, the legal-tender provision is not as unjust in its operation as when applied to past contracts, and does not impair to the same extent private rights. But so far as it makes the receipt of the notes, in absence of any agreement of the parties, compulsory in payment of such contracts, it is, in my judgment, equally unconstitutional. This seems, to me, to follow necessarily from the duty already mentioned cast upon Congress by the coinage power—to create and maintain an uniform metallic standard of value throughout the Union. Without a standard of value of some kind, commerce would be difficult, if not impossible, and just in proportion to the uniformity and stability of the standard, is the security and consequent extent of commercial transactions. How is it possible for Congress to discharge its duty by making the acceptance of paper promises compulsory in all future dealings—promises which necessarily depend for their value upon the confidence entertained by the public in their ultimate payment, and the consequent ability of the holder to convert them into gold or silver—promises which can never be uniform throughout the Union, but must have different values in different portions of the country; one value in New York, another at New Orleans, and still a different one at San Francisco.

Speaking of paper money issued by the States,—and the same language is equally true of paper money issued by the United States,— Chief Justice MARSHALL says, in CRAIG vs. THE STATE OF MISSOURI: "Such a medium has been always liable to considerable fluctuation. Its value is continually changing; and these changes often great and sudden, expose individuals to immense loss, are the sources of ruinous speculations, and destroy all confidence between man and man. To cut up this mischief by the roots, a mischief which was felt through the United States and which deeply affected the interest and prosperity of all, the people declared in their Constitution that no State should emit bills of credit."—(4 *Peters*, 432.)

Mr. Justice WASHINGTON, after referring, in OGDEN *vs.* SAUNDERS (12 *Wheaton*, 265), to the provision of the Constitution declaring that no State shall coin money, emit bills of credit, make anything but gold and silver coin a tender in payment of debts, says: "These prohibitions, associated with the powers granted to Congress 'to coin money and to regulate the value thereof, and of foreign coin,' most obviously constitute members of the same family, being upon the same subject, and governed by the same policy. This policy was, to provide a fixed and uniform standard of value throughout the United States, by which the commercial and other dealings between the citizens thereof, or between them and foreigners, as well as the moneyed transactions of the government, should be regulated. For it might well be asked, why vest in Congress the power to establish a uniform standard of value by the means pointed out, if the States might use the same means, and thus defeat the uniformity of the standard, and consequently the standard itself? And why establish a standard at all for the government of the various contracts which might be entered into, if those contracts might afterwards be discharged by a different standard, or by that which is not money, under the authority of State tender laws? It is obvious, therefore, that these prohibitions in the tenth section are entirely homogeneous, and are essential to the establishment of an uniform standard of value in the formation and discharge of contracts."

It is plain that this policy cannot be carried out, and this fixed and uniform metallic standard of value throughout the United States be maintained, so long as any other standard is attempted, which of itself has no intrinsic value and is forever fluctuating and uncertain.

For the reasons which I have endeavored to unfold, I am compelled to dissent from the judgment of the majority of the court. I know that the measure, the validity of which I have called in question, was passed in the midst of a gigantic rebellion, when even the bravest hearts sometimes doubted the safety of the Republic, and that the patriotic men who adopted it did so under the conviction that it would increase the ability of the government to obtain funds and supplies, and thus advance the national cause. Were I to be governed by my appreciation of the character of those men, instead of my views of the requirements of the Constitution, I should readily assent to the views of the majority of the court. But, sitting as a judicial officer, and bound to compare every law enacted by Congress with the greater law enacted by the people, and being unable to reconcile the measure in question with that fundamental law, I cannot hesitate to pronounce it as being, in my judgment, unconstitutional and void.

In the discussions which have attended this subject of legal-tender there has been at times what seemed to me to be a covert intimation, that opposition to the measure in question was the expression of a spirit not altogether favorable to the cause, in the interest of which that measure was adopted. All such intimations I repel with all the energy I can express. I do not yield to any one in honoring and reverencing the noble and patriotic men who were in the councils of the nation during the terrible struggle with the rebellion. To them belong the greatest of all glories in our history—that of having saved the Union, and that of having emancipated a race. For these results they will be remembered and honored so long as the English language is spoken or read among men. But I do not admit that a blind approval of every measure which they may have thought essential to put down the rebellion is any evidence of loyalty to the country. The only loyalty which I can admit consists in obedience to the Constitution and laws made in pursuance of it. It is only by obedience that affection and reverence can be shown to a superior having a right to command. So thought our great Master when he said to his disciples: " If ye love me, keep my commandments."

THE LEGAL TENDER CASES OF 1871.

DECISION OF THE SUPREME COURT OF THE UNITED STATES.

In addition to the opinions delivered by Justices Strong and Bradley in favor of the constitutionality of the Legal-Tender Act of Congress, and the dissenting opinions of Justices Chase, Clifford and Field, we now publish the cases quoted or referred to in their several opinions. These cases may be considered as the authorities or grounds of the decision given in the above cases at the December Term of 1870, viz.:—

1. Apsden v. Austin, 5 Ad. & Ellis, 671.
2. B. U. S. v. B. S. Geo., 10 Wheat., 333
3. Bank v. Supervisors, 7 Wallace, 26.
4. Barrington v. Potter, Dyer, 81.
5. Briscoe v. B. of Ky., 8 Peters, 118.
6. Bronson v. Rodes, 7 Wallace, 229.
7. Butler v. Horwitz, 7 Wallace, 259.
8. Calder v. Bull, 3 Dallas, 388.
9. Coffin v. Landis, 10 Wright, 426.
10. Cohens v. B. of Va., 6 Wheat., 264.
11. Collector v. Day, 11 Wallace, 113.
12. Commonwealth of Pa. v. Smith, 4 Binney, 123.
13. Craig v. State of Mo., 2 Peters, 410.
14. Dewing v. Sears, 11 Wallace, 379.
15. Dobbins v. Brown, 2 Jones, 75.
16. Dunn v. Sayles, 5 Ad. & Ellis, 685.
17. Faw v. Marsteller, 2 Cranch, 10.
18. Fisher v. U. S., 2 Cranch, 358.
19. Fletcher v. Peck, 6 Cranch, 87.
20. Fox v. St. of Ohio, 5 Howard, 410.
21. Gibbons v. Ogden, 9 Wheaton, 1.
22. Gwin v. Breedlove, 2 Howard, 29.
23. Hepburn v. Griswold, 8 Wall., 603.
24. Lane County v. Oregon, 7 Wall., 73.
25. Martin v. Hunter, 1 Wheaton, 304.
26. Metrop. B. v. V. Dyck, 27 N.Y., 400.
27. McCulloh v. State of Maryland.
28. Milligan, ex parte, 4 Wallace, 120.
29. Noonan v. Bradley, 9 Wallace, 394.
30. Ogden v. Saunders, 12 Wheat., 213.
31. Peck v. Sanderson, 18 Howard, 42.
32. Robinson v. Noble, 8 Peters, 198.
33. Sibbald v. U. States, 12 Peters, 492.
34. Snow v. Perry, 9 Pickering, 542.
35. S. of Texas v. White, 7 Wall., 700.
36. Sturges v. Crowninshield, 4 Wheat., 204.
37. Thorndike v. U. S., 2 Mason, 18.
38. Thompson v. Riggs, 5 Wall., 663.
39. U. S. v. Marigold, 9 Howard, 560.
40. Veazie Bank v. Fenno, 8 Wall., 533.
41. Ward v. S. of Maryland, 12 Wallace.
42. Washington Bridge Co. v. Stewart, 3 Howard.
43. Workman v. Mifflin, 6 Casey, 362.
44. Willard v. Tayloe, 8 Wallace, 568.
45. Wright v. Reid, 3 Term Reports, 554

I. APSDEN vs. AUSTIN. (*Page 21.*)

By an agreement between plaintiff and defendant, plaintiff agreed to manufacture for defendant cement of a certain quality, and defendant, on condition of plaintiff's performing such engagement, promised to pay him £4 weekly during the two years following the date of the agreement, and £5 weekly during the year next following, and also to receive him into partnership as a manufacturer of cement at the expiration of three years ; and plaintiff engaged to instruct defendant in the art of manufacturing cement. Each party bound himself in a penal sum to fulfill the agreement. Defendant afterwards covenanted by deed for the performance of the agreement on his part. *Held*, that the stipulations in the agreement did not raise an implied covenant that defendant should employ plaintiff in the business during three or two years, though defendant was bound by the express words to pay plaintiff the stipulated wages during those periods respectively, if plaintiff performed, or was ready to perform, the condition precedent on his part.—(ASPDIN *vs.* AUSTIN, 5 *Queen's Bench Reports, page* 671.)

II. BANK OF THE U. S. *vs.* BANK OF THE STATE OF GEORGIA.
(*Page* 74.)

In general, a payment received in forged paper, or in any case coin, is not good; and if there be no negligence in the party he may recover back the consideration paid for them, or sue upon his original demand. But this principle does not apply to a payment made *bona fide* to a bank, in its own notes, which are received as cash, and afterwards discovered to be forged. In case of such a payment upon general account, an action may be maintained by the party paying the notes, if there is a balance due him from the bank upon their general account, either upon an *insumul computassent*, or as for money had and received.—(BANK U. S. *vs.* BANK STATE OF GEORGIA, 10 *Wheaton's Reports, page* 333.)

III. BANK OF NEW YORK *vs.* SUPERVISORS. (*Pages* 46, 73.)

United States notes issued under the Loan and Currency Acts of 1862 and 1863, intended to circulate as money, and actually constituting, with the national bank notes, the ordinary circulating medium of the country, are, moreover, obligations of the national government, and exempt from State taxation. United States notes are engagements to pay dollars ; and the dollars intended are coined dollars of the United States.—(BANK OF NEW YORK *vs.* SUPERVISORS, 7 *Wallace's Reports, page* 26.)

IV. BARRINGTON *vs.* POTTER. (*Page* 22.)

Debt against executors for rent accrued after testator's death in the *debet* and *detinet ;* plea, an eviction of part of the land in the testator's life-time, and a tender of the rent for the remainder in shillings ; and demurrer, because the shillings before bringing the action were lowered by proclamation to the value of sixpence only.—BARRINGTON *vs.* POTTER, 1 *Dyer's Reports, page* 81.)

Legal Tender Cases of 1871.

V. BRISCOE vs. COMMONWEALTH BANK OF KENTUCKY
(*Pages* 25, 70, 71.)

In cases where constitutional questions are involved, unless four judges of the court concur in opinion, thus making the decision that of a majority of the whole court, it is not the practice of the court to deliver any judgment, except in cases of absolute necessity. Four judges not having concurred in opinion as to the Constitutional questions argued in these cases, the court directed that the cases shall be re-argued at the next term.—(BRISCOE AND OTHERS vs. THE COMMONWEALTH BANK OF KENTUCKY, 8 *Peters' Reports, page* 118.)

VI. BRONSON vs. RODES. (*Page* 73.)

A bond, given in December, 1851, for payment of a certain sum, in gold and silver coin, lawful money of the United States, with interest also in coin, at a rate specified, until repayment, cannot be discharged by a tender of United States notes issued under the Loan and Currency Acts of 1862 and 1863, and by them declared to be lawful money and a legal tender for the payment of debts. When obligations made payable in coin are sued upon, judgment may be entered for coined dollars and parts of dollars.—(BRONSON vs. RODES, 7 *Wallace's Reports, page* 229.)

VII. BUTLER vs. HORWITZ. (*Page* 73.)

A contract to pay a certain sum in gold and silver coin is in substance and legal effect a contract to deliver a certain weight of gold and silver of a certain fineness to be ascertained by count. Whether the contract be for the delivery or payment of coin or bullion, or other property, damages for non-performance must be assessed in lawful money; that is to say, in money declared to be legal tender in payment, by a law made in pursuance of the Constitution of the United States. There are, at this time, two descriptions of lawful money in use under acts of Congress, in either of which (assuming these acts, in respect to legal tender, to be Constitutional) damages for non-performance of contracts, whether made before or since the passage of these acts may be assessed in the absence of any different understanding or agreement between the parties. When the intent of the parties as to the medium of payment is clearly expressed in a contract, damages for the breach of it, whether made before or since the enactment of these laws, may be properly assessed so as to give effect to that interest. When, therefore, it appears to be the clear intent of a contract that payment for satisfaction shall be made in gold and silver, damages should be assessed in coin, and judgment rendered accordingly.—(BUTLER vs. HORWITZ, 7 *Wallaces' Reports, page* 258.)

116   Notes of Cases.

VIII. CALDER vs. BULL. (Pages 8, 45, 105.)

Upon the whole, though there cannot be a case in which an *ex post facto* law in criminal matters is requisite, or justifiable, yet in the present instance the objection does not arise; because, 1st, if the act of the legislature of Connecticut was a judicial act, it is not within the words of the Constitution; and, 2nd, even if it was a legislative act, it is not within the meaning of the prohibition. This was an appeal from the State of Connecticut.

IX. COFFIN vs. LANDIS. (Page 21.)

Where one as agent for another contracts to sell the lands of the latter, in consideration of one-half the net proceeds of the sales, and there is no stipulation in the contract as to the duration of the employment, the principal has a right to terminate it at any time, and to discharge the agent from his service without notice.—(COFFIN vs. LANDIS, 46 *Pennsylvania State Reports, page* 426.)

X. COHENS vs. STATE OF VIRGINIA. (Page 12.)

The court has, constitutionally, appellate jurisdiction under the judiciary act of 1789, c. 20, s. 25, from the final judgment or decree of the highest court of law or equity of a State, having jurisdiction of the subject matter of the suit, where is drawn in question the validity of a treaty, or statute of, or an authority exercised under, the United States, and the decision is against their validity; or where it is drawn in question, the validity of a statute of, or an authority exercised under, any State, on the ground of their being repugnant to the Constitution, treaties, or laws of the United States, and the decision is in favor of such, validity; or of the Constitution, or of a treaty, or statute of, or commission held under, the United States, and the decision is against the title, right, privilege, or exemption, specially set up or claimed, by either party, under such clause of the Constitution, treaty, statute, or commission. It is no objection to the exercise of this appellate jurisdiction, that one of the parties is a State, and the other a citizen of that State. The act of Congress of the 4th of May, 1812, entitled "An Act further to amend the charter of the City of Washington," which provides (§ 6,) that the Corporation of the City shall be empowered, for certain purposes, and under certain restrictions, to authorize the drawing of lotteries, does not extend to authorize the Corporation to force the sale of the tickets in such lottery, in States where such sale may be prohibited by the State laws.—(COHENS vs. THE STATE OF VIRGINIA, 6 *Wheaton's Reports, page* 264.)

Legal Tender Cases of 1871. 117

XI. THE UNITED STATES *vs.* DAY. (*Page* 66.)

It is not competent for Congress under the Constitution of the United States, to impose a tax upon the salary of a judicial officer of a State.—(THE COLLECTOR *vs.* DAY, 11 *Wallace's Reports, page* 113.)

XII. COMMONWEALTH OF PENNSYLVANIA *vs.* SMITH. (*Page* 10.)

The Supreme Court has no authority to try an issue in fact in any part of the State except the county of Philadelphia; and therefore it cannot in the western district entertain a motion for leave to file an information in nature of a *quo warranto*, because an issue in fact may arise out of it. The sixth section of the fifth article of the Constitution of Pennsylvania does not prohibit the Legislature from taking away, or modifying, the powers before that time usually exercised by the judges of the Supreme Court. It was intended to have an affirmative effect, by introducing certain chancery powers, and not the negative one of prohibiting the taking away of any powers therefor exercised. The Supreme Court exercised no original jurisdiction in civil actions until the year 1785, except as to fines and common recoveries.—(COMMONWEALTH OF PENNSYLVANIA *vs.* SMITH, 4 *Binney's Reports, page* 117.)

XIII. CRAIG *vs.* STATE OF MISSOURI. (*Pages* 70, 110.)

On the 27th day of June, 1821, the legislature of the State of Missouri passed an act, entitled "an act for the establishment of loan offices," by the third section of which the officers of the treasury of the State, under the direction of the governor, were required to issue certificates to the amount of two hundred thousand dollars, of denominations not exceeding ten dollars, nor less than fifty cents, in the following form :

"This certificate shall be receivable at the treasury of any of the loan offices in the State of Missouri, in discharge of taxes or debts due to the State, for the sum of —— dollars, with interest for the same, at the rate of two per centum per annum from this date." These certificates were to be receivable at the treasury, and by tax gatherers and other public officers, in payment of taxes, or moneys due or to become due to the State, or to any town or county therein, and by all officers, civil and military, in the State, in discharge of salaries and fees of office; and in payment for salt made at the salt springs owned by the state, and to be afterwards leased by the authority of the legislature. The twenty-third section of the act pledges certain property of the State for the redemption of these certificates; and the law authorizes the governor to negotiate a loan of silver or gold for the same purpose. A provision is made in the law for the gradual withdrawal of the certificates from circulation; and all the certificates have since been redeemed. The commissioners of the loan offices were authorized to make loans of the certificates to citizens of the State, assigning to each district a proportion of the amount of the certificates, to be secured by mortgage or personal security; the loans to bear interest not exceeding six per cent. per annum, and the loans on personal property to be for less than two hundred dollars. *Held*, that the certificates issued under the authority of the law of Missouri, were "bills of credit;" and that their emission was prohibited by the Constitution of the United States, which declares that no State shall "emit bills of credit." A promissory note given for certificates issued at the loan office of Chariton, in Missouri, payable to the State of Missouri, under the act of the legislature "establishing loan offices," is void. The action was assumpsit on a promissory note, and the record stated "that neither party having required a jury, the cause was submitted to the court, and the court having seen and heard the evidence, the court found that the defendants did assume as the plaintiff had declared; that the consideration for the note and the assumpsit was for loan office certificates, loaned by the State of Missouri at her loan office in Chariton, which certificates were issued under "an act for establishing loan offices," &c. *Held*, that it could not be doubted that the declaration is on a note given in pursuance of the act of Missouri, and that under the plea of assumpsit the defendants were at liberty to question the validity of the consideration which was the foundation of the contract, and the constitutionality of the law in which it originated. The record, thus exhibiting the case, gives jurisdiction to this court over the case, on a writ of error prosecuted by the defendants to this court from the Supreme court of Missouri, under the provisions of the twenty-fifth section of the judiciary act of 1789. Everything which disaffirms the contract; every thing which shows it to be void, may be given in evidence on the general issue in an action of assumpsit. In its enlarged and, perhaps, liberal sense, the term "bill of credit," may comprehend any instrument by which a State engages to pay money at a future day, thus including a certificate given for money borrowed. But the language of the Constitution itself, and the mischief to be prevented, equally limit the interpretation of the terms. The word "emit" is never employed in describing those contracts by which a State binds itself to pay money at a future day for services actually received, or for money borrowed for present use. Nor are instruments executed for such purposes, in common language, denominated "bills of credit." "To emit bills of credit," conveys to the mind the idea of issuing paper intended to circulate throughout the community for its ordinary purposes, as money; which paper is redeemable at a future day. This is the sense in which the terms have always been understood. The Constitution considers the emission of bills of credit and the enactment of tender laws as distinct operations, independent of each other, which may be separately performed. Both are forbidden. To sustain the one because it is not also the other; to say that bills of credit may be emitted, if they be not made a tender in payment of debts, is, in effect, to expunge that distinct independent prohibition, and to read the clause as if it had been entirely omitted. It has been long settled that a promise made in consideration of an act which is forbidden by the law, is void. It will not be questioned that an act forbidden by the Constitution of the United States, which is the supreme law, is against law.—(CRAIG ET AL. *vs.* THE STATE OF MISSOURI, 4 *Peters' Reports, page* 410.)

XIV. DEWING *vs.* SEARS. (*Page* 74.)

On a lease where a yearly rent of "four ounces, two pennyweights, and twelve grains of pure gold in coined money," is reserved, (equivalent, at the time when the lease was made, to $80 per annum, and at the time when suit was brought to $87.25 per annum), judgment should be entered for coined dollars and parts of coined dollars, and not for United States notes, (made by statutes of the United States a legal tender), and equivalent in market value to the value in coined money of the stipulated weight of pure gold.—(DEWING *vs.* SEARS, 11 *Wallace's Reports, page* 379.)

XV. DOBBINS *vs.* BROWN. (*Page* 22.)

A covenant of warranty "against the grantor and his heirs, and against all and every other person or persons lawfully claiming or to claim," is not broken by the entry and occupancy of the Commonwealth, in the exercise of its right of eminent domain. Such entry and occupancy do not amount to an eviction of the ground taken for public use. A release of damages for such entry and occupancy, executed before the conveyance with warranty, is not an eviction. It merely forestalled the compensation, and is a clog on the enjoyment.—(DOBBINS *vs.* BROWN, 12 *Pennsylvania State Reports, page* 75.)

XVI. DUNN *vs.* SAYLES. (*Page* 21.)

Declaration in covenant stated that, by and between defendant, D., and plaintiff, plaintiff covenanted that D. should, for five years from the date, serve defendant in the art of a surgeon dentist, and attend for nine hours each day; and defendant, in consideration of the services to be done by D., covenanted with plaintiff that he, defendant, would, during the five years, (in case D. should faithfully perform his part of the agreement, particularly as to the nine hours, but not otherwise), pay D. 35s. per week for the first year, £2 per week for the second and third, and £2 2s. per week for the fourth and fifth: that D. was in the service for some time after the making of the deed, till dismissed, and during all that faithfully performed service, &c., and was willing and tendered to perform, &c., to the end of the five years; but defendant, during the term, refused to permit D. to remain in his service, and dismissed him. *Held*, on motion in arrest of judgment, that the declaration did not show any covenant corresponding to the breach.—(DUNN *vs.* SAYLES, 5 *Queen's Bench Reports, page* 685.)

XVII. FAW *vs.* MARSTELLER. (*Pages* 22, 99.)

In a deed made in the year 1779, of land rendering an annual rent of £26 *current money of Virginia* forever, the rents are not to be reduced by the scale of depreciation, but the actual annual value of the land, at the date of the contract, in *specie*, or in other money equivalent thereto, is to be ascertained by a jury.—(FAW *vs.* MARSTELLER, 2 *Cranch's Reports, page* 10.

XVIII. FISHER *vs.* BLIGHT. (*Page* 14.)

In all cases of insolvency or bankruptcy of a debtor of the United States, they are entitled to priority of payment out of his effects.— (FISHER *vs.* BLIGHT, 2 *Cranch's Supreme Court Reports, page* 358.)

XIX. FLETCHER *vs.* PECK. (*Pages* 10, 44.)

If the breach of covenant assigned be, that the State had no authority to sell and dispose of the land, it is not a good plea in bar to say that the governor was legally empowered to sell and convey the premises, although the facts stated in the plea as inducement, are sufficient to justify a direct negative of the breach assignment. It is not necessary that a breach of covenant be assigned in the very words of the covenant. It is sufficient if it show a substantial breach; the court will not declare a law to be unconstitutional, unless the opposition between the Constitution and the law be clear and plain. The legislature of Georgia, in 1795, had the power of disposing of the unappropriated lands within its own limits. In a contest between two individuals, claiming under an act of a legislature, the court cannot inquire into the motives which actuated the members of that legislature. If the legislature might constitutionally pass such an act; if the act be clothed with all the requisite forms of a law, a court, sitting as a court of law, cannot sustain a suit between individuals founded on the allegation that the act is a nullity in consequence of the impure motives which influenced certain members of the legislature, which passed the law. When a law is in its nature a contract, when absolute rights have vested under that contract, a repeal of the law cannot divest those rights. A party to a contract cannot pronounce its own deed invalid, although that party be a foreign State. *A grant is a contract executed.* A law annulling conveyances, is unconstitutional, because it is a law impairing the obligation of contracts, within the meaning of the Constitution of the United States. The proclamation of the King of Great Britain, in 1763, did not alter the boundaries of Georgia. The nature of the Indian title is not such as to be absolutely repugnant to seizure in fee on the part of the State.—(FLETCHER vs. PECK, 6 Cranch's Reports, page 87.)

XX. FOX vs. THE STATE OF OHIO. (Page 70.)

The power conferred upon Congress by the fifth and sixth clauses of the eighth section of the first article of the Constitution of the United States, viz: "To coin money, regulate the value thereof, and of foreign coin, and fix the standard of weights and measures;" "to provide for the punishment of counterfeiting the securities and current coin of the United States," does not prevent a State from passing a law to punish the offence of circulating counterfeit coin of the United States. The two offences of counterfeiting the coin, and passing counterfeit money, are essentially different in their characters. The former is an offence directly against the government, by which individuals may be affected; the latter is a private wrong, by which the government may be remotely, if it will in any degree, be reached. The prohibitions contained in the amendments to the Constitution were intended to be restrictions upon the federal government, and not upon the authority of the States.—(FOX vs. THE STATE OF OHIO, 5 Howard's Reports, page 410.)

XXI. GIBBONS vs. OGDEN. (Page 23.)

The acts of the Legislature of the State of New York, granting to ROBERT R. LIVINGSTON and ROBERT FULTON, the exculsive navigation of all the waters within the jurisdiction of that State, with boats moved by fire or steam, for a term of years, are repugnant to that clause of the Constitution of the United States, which authorizes Congress to regulate commerce, so far as the said acts prohibit vessels licensed, according to the laws of the United States, for carrying on the coasting trade, from navigating the said waters by means of fire or steam.—(GIBBONS vs. OGDEN, 9 Wheaton's Reports, page 1.)

XXII. GWIN vs. BREEDLOVE. (Pages 47, 69, 70, 97.)

A statute of the State of Mississippi, passed on the 15th of February, 1828, provided that if a sheriff should fail to pay over to a plaintiff money collected by execution, the amount collected, with twenty-five per cent. damages and eight per cent. interest, might be recovered against such sheriff and his sureties, by motion before the court to which such execution was returnable. A marshal and his sureties cannot be proceeded against jointly, in this summary way, but they must be sued as directed by the Act of Congress. But the marshal himself was always liable to an attachment, under which he could be compelled to bring the money into court; and, by the process act of Congress of May, 1828, was also liable, in Mississippi, to have a judgment entered against himself by motion. This motion is not a new suit, but an incident of the prior one; and hence, residence of the parties in different States need not be averred in order to give jurisdiction to the court. Such parts only of the laws of a State as are applicable to the courts of the United States are adopted by the process act of Congress; a penalty is not adopted, and the twenty-five per cent. damages cannot be enforced. A marshal who receives bank notes in satisfaction of an execution, when the return has not been set aside at the instance of the plaintiff, or amended by the marshal himself, must account to the plaintiff in gold or silver; the Constitution of the United States recognizing only gold and silver as a legal tender.—(GWIN vs. BREEDLOVE, 2 *Howard's U. S. Reports, page* 29.

XXIII. HEPBURN vs. GRISWOLD. (*Pages* 16, 36, 37, 39, 41, 57, 58, 60, 68, 81, 91, 100, 109.)

Construed by the plain import of their terms and the manifest intent of the legislature, the statutes of 1862 and 1863, which make United States notes a legal tender in payment of debts, public and private, apply to debts contracted before as well as to debts contracted after enactment. When a case arises for judicial determination, and the decision depends on the alleged inconsistency of a legislative provision with the Constitution, it is the plain duty of the Supreme court to compare the act with the fundamental law, and if the former cannot, upon a fair construction, be reconciled with the latter, to give effect to the Constitution rather than the statute. There is in the Constitution no express grant of legislative power to make any description of credit currency a legal tender in payment of debts. The words "all laws necessary and proper for carrying into execution" powers expressly granted or vested, have, in the Constitution, a sense equivalent to that of the words, laws not absolutely necessary indeed, but appropriate, plainly adapted to constitutional and legitimate ends, which are not prohibited, but consistent with the letter and spirit of the Constitution; laws really calculated to effect objects intrusted to the government. Among means appropriate, plainly adapted, not inconsistent with the spirit of the Constitution, nor prohibited by its terms, the legislature has unrestricted choice; but no power can be derived by implication from any express power to enact laws as means for carrying it into execution, unless such laws come within this description. The making of notes or bills of credit a legal tender in payment of pre-existing debts, is not a means appropriate, plainly adapted, or really calculated to carry into effect any express power vested in Congress, is inconsistent with the spirit of the Constitution, and is prohibited by the Constitution. The clause in the acts of 1862 and 1863, which makes United States notes a legal tender in payment of all debts, public and private, is, so far as it applies to debts contracted before the passage of those acts, unwarranted by the Constitution. Prior to the 25th of February, 1862, all contracts for the payment of money, not expressly stipulating otherwise, were, in legal effect and universal understanding, contracts for the payment of coin; and, under the Constitution, the parties to such contracts are respectively entitled to demand and bound to pay the sums due, according to their terms, in coin, notwithstanding the clause in that act, and the subsequent acts of like tenor, which make United States notes a legal tender in payment of such debts.—(HEPBURN *vs.* GRISWOTD, 8 *Wallace's Reports, page* 603.)

XXIV. LANE COUNTY *vs.* OREGON. (*Page* 74.)

An enactment in a State statute that " the sheriff shall pay over to the county treasurer the full amount of the State and school taxes, in gold and silver coin," and that " the several county treasurers shall pay over to the State treasurer the State tax, in gold and silver coin," requires by legitimate, if not necessary, consequence that the taxes named be *collected* in coin. But if in the judgment of this court this were otherwise, yet the Supreme Court of the State having held this construction to be correct, this court will follow their adjudication. The clauses in the several acts of Congress, of 1862 and 1863, making United States notes a legal tender for debts, have no reference to taxes imposed by State authority.—(7 *Wallace's Reports, page* 71.)

XXV. MARTIN *vs.* HUNTER. (*Pages* 11, 75, 101.)

The appellate jurisdiction of the Supreme Court of the United States extends to a final judgment or decree in any suit in the highest court of law or equity of a State; where is drawn in question the validity of a treaty, or statute of, or an authority exercised under, the United States, and the decision is against their validity; or where is drawn in question the validity of a statute of, or an authority exercised under, any State, on the ground of their being repugnant to the Constitution, treaties, or laws of the United States, and the decision is in favor of such their validity, or the construction of a treaty, or statute of, or commission held under, the United States, and the decision is against the title, rights, privilege, or execution specially set up or claimed, by either party, under such clause of the Constitution, treaty, statute, or commission. Such judgment or decree may be reexamined by writ of error in the same manner as if rendered in a circuit court. If the cause has been once rendered before, and the State court decline or refuse to carry into effect the mandate of the supreme court thereon, this court will proceed to a final decision of the same, and award execution thereon. If the validity or construction of a treaty of the United States is drawn in question, and the decision is against its validity, or the title specially set up by either party, under the treaty, this court has jurisdiction to ascertain that title and determine its legal validity, and is not confined to the abstract construction of the treaty itself. The return of a copy of the record, under the seal of the court, certified by the clerk, and annexed to the writ of error, is a sufficient return in such a case. It need not appear that the judge who granted the writ of error did, upon issuing the citation, take a bond, as required by the 22nd section of the judiciary act. That provision is merely directory to the judge, and the presumption of law is, until the contrary appears, that every judge who signs a citation has obeyed the injunctions of the act.— (MARTIN vs. HUNTER'S LESSEE, 1 *Wheaton's Reports, page* 304.)

XXVI. METROPOLITAN BANK vs. VAN DYCK. (*Page* 64.)

The act of Congress, passed February 25th, 1862 (ch. 33), making certain treasury notes of the United States a legal tender in payment of debts between private persons, is constitutional and valid. The power to borrow money on the credit of the United States carries with it, it seems, the power to attach the quality of a legal tender to the notes issued, when, in the judgment of Congress, it is necessary to make them effectual for the purpose of borrowing. The provision of the Constitution of this State (art. 8, sec. 6) that the legislature shall require the redemption in specie of all bills and notes put in circulation as money, is not self-executing, so that the refusal of a bank to redeem its bills in specie authorizes the bank superintendent to sell the securities deposited with him. Until the legislature shall require the redemption of bank bills in specie, an offer to pay in treasury notes, made a legal tender by act of Congress, is sufficient under the general banking law (ch. 260 of 1838, sec. 4), which only authorizes a sale of the securities upon default in paying such bills in "lawful money of the United States."—(METROPOLITAN BANK vs. VAN DYCK, 27 *New York Reports, page* 400.)

XXVII. McCULLOH vs. THE STATE OF MARYLAND.
(*Pages* 11, 14, 15, 17, 35, 37, 39, 66, 75, 78, 86.)

Congress has power to incorporate a bank. The government of the Union is a government of the people; it emanates from them; its powers are granted by them; and are to be exercised directly on them, and for their benefit. The government of the Union, though limited in its powers, is supreme within its sphere of action; and its laws, when made in pursuance of the constitution, form the supreme law of the land. There is nothing in the Constitution of the United States similar to the articles of confederation, which exclude incidental or implied powers. If the end be legitimate and within the scope of the constitution, all the *means* which are appropriate, which are plainly adapted to that *end,* and which are not prohibited, may constitutionally be employed to carry it into effect. The power of establishing a corporation is not a distinct sovereign power or end of government, but only the means of carrying into effect other powers which are sovereign. Whenever it becomes an appropriate means of exercising any of the powers given by the Constitution to the government of the Union, it may be exercised by that government. If a certain means to carry into effect any of the powers expressly given by the Constitution to the government of the Union, be an appropriate measure, not prohibited by the Constitution, the degree of its necessity is a question of legislative discretion, not of judicial cognizance. The act of the 10th April, 1816, sec. 44, to "incorporate the subscribers to the Bank of the United States," is a law made in pursuance of the Constitution. The Bank of the United States has, constitutionally, a right to establish its branches or offices of discount and deposit within any State. The State, within which such branches may be established, cannot, without violating the Constitution, tax that branch. The State governments have no right to tax any of the constitutional means employed by the government of the Union to execute its constitutional powers. The States have no power by taxation, or otherwise, to retard, impede, burden, or in any manner control, the operations of the constitutional laws enacted by Congress, to carry into effect the powers vested in the national government. This principle does not extend to a tax paid by the real property of the Bank of the United States in common with the other real property in a particular State, nor to a tax imposed on the proprietary interest which the citizens of that State may hold in this institution, in common with other property of the same description throughout the State.—McCULLOH vs. THE STATE OF MARYLAND ET AL., 4 *Wheaton's Reports, page* 316.

XXVIII. *Ex parte* MILLIGAN. (*Page* 79.)

Circuit courts, as well as the judges thereof, are authorized by the fourteenth section of the Judiciary act, to issue the writ *habeas* for the purpose of inquiring into the cause of commitment, and they have jurisdiction, except in cases where the privilege of the writ is suspended, to hear and determine the question whether the party is entitled to be discharged. The usual course of proceeding is for the court, on the application of the prisoner for a writ of *habeas corpus,* to issue the writ, and on its return to hear and dispose of the case; but where the cause of imprisonment is fully shown by the petition, the court may, without issuing the writ, consider and determine whether upon the facts presented in the petition, the prisoner, if brought before the court, would be discharged. When the circuit court renders a final judgment refusing to discharge the prisoner, he may bring the case here by writ of error; and if the judges of the circuit court, being opposed in opinion, can render no judgment, he may have the point upon which the disagreement happens certified to this tribunal. A petition for a writ of *habeas corpus,* duly presented, is the institution of a cause on behalf of the petitioner; and the allowance or refusal of the process, as well as the subsequent disposition of the prisoner, matter of law and not of discretion. A person arrested after the passage of the act of March 3d, 1863, "relating to *habeas corpus*, and regulating judicial proceedings in certain cases," and under the authority of the said act, was entitled to his discharge, if not indicted or presented by the grand jury convened at the first subsequent term of the circuit or district court of the United States for the district. The omission to furnish a list of the persons arrested, to the judges of the circuit or district court as provided in the said act, did not impair the right of such person, if not indicted or presented, to his discharge. Military commissions organized during the late civil war, in a State not invaded and not engaged in rebellion, in which the federal courts were open, and in the proper and unobstructed exercise of their judicial functions, had no jurisdiction to try, convict or sentence for any criminal offence, a citizen who was neither a resident of a rebellious State, nor a prisoner of war, nor a person in the military or naval service. And Congress could not invest them with any such power. The guaranty of trial by jury contained in the Constitution was intended for a state of war as well as a state of peace; and is equally binding upon rulers and people at all times and under all circumstances. The federal authority having been unopposed in the State of Indiana, and the federal courts open for the trial of offences and the redress of grievances, the usages of war could not, under the Constitution, afford any sanction for the trial there of a citizen in civil life, not connected with the military or naval service, by a military tribunal, for any offence whatever. Cases arising in the land or naval forces or the militia in time of war or public danger, are excepted from the necessity of presentment or indictment by a grand jury; and the right of trial by jury, in such cases, is subject to the same exceptions. Neither the President nor Congress, nor the judiciary can disturb any one of the safeguards of civil liberty incorporated into the Constitution, except so far the right is given to suspend in certain cases the privilege of the writ of *habeas corpus*. A citizen not connected with the military service and resident in the State where the courts are open and in the proper exercise of their jurisdiction, cannot, even when the privilege of the writ of *habeas corpus* is suspended, be tried, convicted or sentenced, otherwise than by the ordinary courts of law. Suspension of the privilege of the writ of *habeas corpus* does not suspend the writ itself. The writ issues as a matter of course; and on its return the court decides whether the applicant is denied the right of proceeding any further. A person who is a resident of a loyal State where he was arrested, who was never resident in any State engaged in rebellion, nor connected with the military or naval service, cannot be regarded as a prisoner of war.—(*Ex parte* MILLIGAN, 4 *Wallace's Reports, page* 2.)

XXIX. NOONAN *vs.* BRADLEY. (*Page* 60.)

An administrator appointed in one State cannot, by virtue of such appointment, maintain an action in another State, in the absence of a statute of the latter State giving effect to that appointment, to enforce an obligation due his intestate. If he desires to prosecute a suit in another State he must first obtain a grant of administration therein in accordance with its laws. In an action by a plaintiff as an administrator, the objection that, as to the causes of action stated in the declaration, he is not, and never has been, administrator of the effects of the deceased, may be taken by a special plea in bar. *It would appear* that the objection may also be taken by a plea in abatement. One plea in bar is not waived by the existence of another plea in bar, though the two may be inconsistent in their averments with each other. The remedy of the plaintiff in such case is not by demurrer, but by motion to strike out one of the pleas, or to compel the defendant to elect by which he will abide. In an action by a plaintiff as administrator, a plea to the merits admits the representative character of the plaintiff to the extent stated in the declaration, and if that statement is consistent with the grant of letters within the State, it also admits his right to sue in that capacity;—but such a plea admits nothing more than the title stated in the declaration. The substitution in this court of an administrator as a party in place of his intestate on the record, in a case pending on appeal, only authorizes the prosecution of that case in his name; it confers no right to prosecute any other suit in his name. In an action in one State by an administrator appointed in another State, on a bond given to the intestate, a plea that the bond was *bona notabilia* on the death of the decedent, in the State other than the one which appointed the administrator suing as plaintiff, and that an administrator of the effects of the decedent in that State has been appointed and qualified is a good answer to the action. It is an averment of facts which in law excludes all right to, and control over, the property in that State by the foreign administrator. Where a bond for the purchase-money of certain land was delivered upon an agreement indorsed upon the bond by the obligee that he would not enforce the bond in case his title to the land should fail: *Held*, that the agreement was not limited in its operation to the time when the bond matured or the penalty became forfeited, but was a perpetual covenant not to enforce the bond in case the designated event at any time happened. Where doubts exist as to the construction of an instrument prepared by one party, upon the faith of which the other party has incurred obligations or parted with his property, that construction should be adopted which will be favorable to the latter party; and where an instrument is susceptible of two constructions—the one working injustice and the other consistent with the right of the case—that one should be favored which upholds the right. The agreement above-mentioned indorsed on the bond constitutes a part of the condition of the bond, qualifying its provisions for the payment of the instalments of the principal and interest, and declaring in effect, that the payments shall not be required, and the obligation of the bond shall cease in case the event designated happens.—(NOONAN *vs.* BRADLEY, 9 *Wallace's Reports*, page 394.)

XXX. OGDEN vs. SAUNDERS. (*Page* 70.)

The power of Congress "*to establish uniform laws on the subject of bankruptcies throughout the* UNITED STATES," does not exclude the right of the States to legislate on the same subject, except when the power is actually exercised by Congress, and the State laws conflict with those of Congress. A bankrupt or insolvent law of any State, which discharges both the person of the debtor and his future acquisitions of property, is not "a law impairing the obligation of contracts," so far as respects debts contracted subsequent to the passage of such law. But a certificate of discharge, under such a law, cannot be pleaded in bar of an action brought by a citizen of another State, in the Courts of the United States, or of any other State than that where the discharge was obtained.—(OGDEN *vs.* SAUNDERS, 12 *Wheaton's Reports, page* 213.)

XXXI. PECK vs. SANDERSON. (*Page* 60.)

This court cannot grant a motion for the re-hearing of a cause which has been transmitted to the court below.—(PECK *vs.* SANDERSON, 18 *Howard's Reports, page* 42.)

XXXII. ROBINSON vs. NOBLE. (*Page* 74.)

N. stipulated in certain articles of agreement to transport and deliver, by the steamboat Paragon, to K., a certain quantity of subsistence stores, supposed to amount to seven hundred barrels, for the use of the United States: in consideration whereof R. agreed to pay to N., on the delivery of the stores at St. Louis, at a certain rate per barrel, one-half in specie funds, or their equivalent, and the other half to be paid in Cincinnati, in the paper of banks current there at the period of the delivery of the stores at St. Louis. Under the agreement was the following memorandum: "It is understood that the payment to be made in Cincinnati, is to be in the paper of the Miami Exporting Company, or its equivalent." The court erred in refusing to instruct the jury that the plaintiffs could only recover the stipulated price for the freight actually transported, and that they were entitled to no more than the specie value of the notes of the Miami Exporting Company Bank, at the time the payment should have been made at Cincinnati. The specie value of the notes, at the time they should have been paid, is the rule by which such damages are to be estimated. The plaintiff, the owner of the steamboat, was not entitled under the contract to recover in damages more than the stipulated price for the freight actually transported. If R. had bound himself to deliver a certain number of barrels, and had failed to do so, N. would have been entitled to damages for such failure; but a fair construction of the contract imposed no such obligation on R. There is no pretence that R. did not deliver the whole amount of freight in his possession at the places designated in the contract. In this respect, as well as in every other, in regard to the contract, he seems to have acted in good faith; and he was unable to deliver the number of barrels supposed, either through the loss stated, or an erroneous estimate of the quantity. But, to exonerate R. from damages on this ground, it is enough to know that he did not bind himself to deliver any specific amount of freight. The probable amount is stated, or supposed, in the agreement, but there is no undertaking as to the quantity.—(ROBINSON vs. NOBLE'S ADMINISTRATORS, 8 *Peters' Reports, page* 181.)

XXXIII. SIBBALD vs. THE UNITED STATES. (*Page* 33.)

On an appeal from the superior court of East Florida by the United States, the decree of the court of East Florida was in part affirmed; the title of SIBBALD, the appellee, to whom the grant of land had been made by the Spanish Governor, before the cession of Florida, having been deemed valid by the Supreme court. The decree of the Supreme court directed the surveyor of public lands in East Florida to do all things enjoined on him by law, in relation to the lands in the surveys made for the grantee. The case was remanded to the Superior court of East Florida for the execution of this decree. The mandate of the supreme court for the execution of the decree of the supreme court was directed to the superior court of East Florida, and the surveyor of public lands would not make the surveys of the lands in the grant according to the decision of the court, the mandate having not been issued to him. A petition was presented to the court by SIBBALD, stating these facts, and asking the court to order that a mandate be made out, directing the surveyor of public lands to do all required of him in relation to the surveys of the lands of the grantee in conformity with the decree of the court; and also to the Superior court of East Florida, directing the court to cause further to be done therein what of right according to law and justice, and in conformity to the decree of the court, ought to be done. *By the Court:*—Had it appeared that a mandate more special than the one which was sent would have been necessary, it would have been ordered. The court is bound to grant a mandate which will suit the case. The mandate which is annexed to the petition, was issued by the clerk, directed only to the court below, and no direction is given to the surveyor. It is, therefore, no execution of the final decree of the Supreme court; and as it remains unexecuted, it is not too late to have it done; and requires no new order or decree in any way modifying that which has been rendered. The clerk was ordered to make out a certificate of the final decree of the court before rendered; and also a mandate according to such final decree, the opinion of the court in the case, and on the petition. Appellate power is exercised over the proceedings of inferior courts, not on those of the appellate courts. The Superior court have no power to review their decisions whether in a case at law or equity. A final decree in chancery is as conclusive as a judgment of law. Both are conclusive on the rights of the parties thereby adjudicated. No principle is better settled, or of more universal application, that no court can reverse or annul its own final decrees or judgments for errors of fact or law after the term in which they have been rendered, unless for clerical mistakes; or to reinstate a cause, dismissed by mistake; from which it follows, that no change or modification can be made which substantially vary or affect it in any material thing. Bills of review in cases of equity, and writs of errors, *coram vobis*, at law are exceptions. When the Supreme court have executed their power in a case before them, and their final decree or judgment requires some further act to be done, it cannot issue an execution, but will send a special mandate to the court below to award it. Whatever was before the court and is disposed of, is considered finally settled. The inferior court is bound by the decree, as the law of the case, and must carry it into execution according to the mandate; they can examine it for no other purpose than execution; or give any other or further relief; or review it upon any matter decided on appeal for error apparent; or intermeddle with it further than to settle so much as has been remanded. After a mandate, no re-hearing will be granted; and on a subsequent appeal, nothing is brought up but the proceeding subsequent to the mandate. If the special mandate directed by the 24th section of the judiciary act is not obeyed, then the general power given to "all the courts of the United States to issue any writs which are necessary for the exercise of their respective jurisdictions, and agreeable to the principles and usages of the law," by the 14th section of judiciary act, fairly arises; and a mandamus or other appropriate writ will go.—(*Ex parte* SIBBALD *vs*. THE UNITED STATES, 12 *Peters' Reports, page* 488.)

XXXIV. SNOW *vs*. PERRY. (*Page* 74.)

Where the maker of a promissory note sent bills of a certain bank to the payee, with instructions to the messenger to see that the amount was indorsed on the note, or to take a receipt, and the payee took the bills, and gave a receipt by which he promised to indorse the amount or return the bills when called for; and the next day, and before the maker had notice of this conditional receipt, the bank failed, it was *held*, that the taking of the bills was a payment *pro tanto*, the messenger being a special agent, and having exceeded his authority in taking a conditional receipt.—(SNOW *vs*. PERRY, 9 *Pickering's Reports, page* 539.)

XXXV. STATE OF TEXAS *vs*. WHITE. (*Page* 35.)

The word STATE describes sometimes a people or community of individuals united more or less closely in political relations, inhabiting temporarily or permanently the same country; often it denotes only the country, or territorial region, inhabited by such a community; not unfrequently it is applied to the government under which the people live; at other times, it represents the combined idea of people, territory, and government. In the Constitution, the term State most frequently expresses the combined idea just noticed, of people, territory, and government. A State, in the ordinary sense of the Constitution, is a political community of free citizens, occupying a territory of defined boundaries, and organized under a government sanctioned and limited by a written constitution, and established by the consent of the governed. But the term is also used to express the idea of a people or political community, as distinguished from the government. In this sense it is used in the clause which provides that the United States shall guarantee to every State in the Union a republican form of government, and shall protect each of them against invasion. The union of the States never was a purely artificial, arbitrary relation. It began among the colonies, and grew out of common origin, mutual sympathies, kindred principles, similar interests, and geographical relations. It was confirmed and strengthened by the necessities of war, and received definite form, and character, and sanction, from the articles of confederation. By these the union was solemnly declared to "be perpetual." And, when these articles were found to be inadequate to the exigencies of the country, the Constitution was ordained " to form a more perfect union." But the perpetuity and indissolubility of the union by no means implies the loss of distinct and individual existence, or of the right of self-government by the States. On the contrary, it may be not unreasonably said, that the preservation of the States, and the maintenance of their governments, are as much within the design and care of the Constitution as the preservation of the Union and the maintenance of the national government. The Constitution, in all its provisions, looks to an indestructible union, composed of indestructible States. When Texas became one of the United States, she entered into an indissoluble relation. The union between Texas and the other States was as complete, as perpetual, and as indissoluble, as the union between the original States. There was no place for reconsideration or revocation, except through revolution or through consent of the States.

Considered as transactions under the Constitution, the ordinance of secession, adopted by the convention and ratified by a majority of the citizens of Texas, and all the acts of her legislature intended to give effect to that ordinance, were absolutely null. They were utterly without operation in law. The State did not cease to be a State, nor her citizens to be citizens of the Union. But in order to the exercise, by a State, of the right to sue in this court, there needs to be a State government, competent to represent the State in its relations with the national government, so far, at least, as the institution and prosecution of a suit are concerned. While Texas was controlled by a government hostile to the United States, and in affiliation with a hostile confederation, waging war upon the United States, no suit, instituted in her name, could be maintained in this court. It was necessary that the government and the people of the State should be restored to peaceful relations to the United States, under the Constitution, before such a suit could be prosecuted. Authority to suppress rebellion is found in the power to suppress insurrection and carry on war; and authority to provide for the restoration of State governments, under the Constitution, when subverted and overthrown, is derived from the obligation of the United States to guarantee to every State in the Union a republican form of government. The latter, indeed, in the case of a rebellion which involves the government of a State, and for the time excludes the national authority from its limits, seems to be a necessary complement to the other. When slavery was abolished, the new freemen necessarily became part of the people, and the people still constituted the State; for States, like individuals, retain their identity, though changed, to some extent, in their constituent elements. And it was the State, thus constituted, which was now entitled to the benefit of the constitutional guaranty. In the exercise of the power conferred by the guaranty clause, as in the exercise of every other constitutional power, a discretion in the choice of means is necessarily allowed. It is essential only that the means must be necessary and proper for carrying into execution the power conferred, through the restoration of the State to its constitutional relations, under a republican form of government; and that no acts be done, and no authority exerted, which is either prohibited or unsanctioned by the Constitution. So long as the war continued, it cannot be denied that the President might institute temporary government within insurgent districts occupied by the national forces, or take provisional measures, in any State, for the restoration of State government faithful to the Union, employing, however, in such efforts, only such means and agents as were authorized by constitutional laws. But, the power to carry into effect the clause of guaranty is primarily a legislative power, and resides in Congress, though necessarily limited to cases where the rightful government is subverted by revolutionary violence, or in imminent danger of being overthrown by an opposing government, set up by force within the State. The several executives of Texas, partially, at least, re-organized under the authority of the President and of Congress, having sanctioned this suit, the necessary conclusion is, that it was instituted and is prosecuted by competent authority. Public property of a State, alienated during rebellion by an usurping State government for the purpose of carrying on war against the United States, may be reclaimed by a restored State government, organized in allegiance to the Union, for the benefit of the State. Exact definitions, within which the acts of a State government, organized in hostility to the Constitution and government of the United States, must be treated as valid or invalid, need not be attempted. It may be said, however, that acts necessary to peace and good order among citizens, such, for example, as acts sanctioning and protecting marriage and the domestic relations, governing the course of descents, regulating the conveyance and the transfer of property, real and personal, and providing remedies for injuries to person and estate, and other similar acts, which would be valid if emanating from a lawful government, must be regarded in general as valid when proceeding from an actual, though unlawful, government; and that acts in furtherance or support of rebellion against the United States, or intended to defeat the just rights of citizens, and other acts of like nature, must, in general, be regarded as invalid and void. Purchasers of United States bonds issued payable to the State of Texas or bearer, alienated during rebellion by the insurgent government, and acquired after the date at which the bonds became redeemable, are affected with notice of defect of title in the seller.—(THE STATE OF TEXAS *vs.* WHITE, 7 *Wallace's Reports, page* 700.)

XXXVI. STURGES *vs.* CROWNINSHIELD. (*Page* 70, 71, 103.)

Since the adoption of the Constitution of the United States, a State has authority to pass a bankrupt law, provided such law does not impair the obligation of contracts within the meaning of the Constitution, art. 1, sec. 10, and provided there be no act of Congress in force to establish a uniform system of bankruptcy, conflicting with such law. The act of the legislature of the State of New York, passed on the 3d of April, 1811, (which not only liberates the person of the debtor, but discharges him from all liability for any debt contracted previous to his discharge, on his surrendering his property in the manner it prescribes,) so far as it attempts to discharge the contract, is a law impairing the obligation of contracts within the meaning of the Constitution of the United States, and is not a good plea in bar of an action brought upon such contract.—(STURGES *vs.* CROWNINSHIELD, 4 *Wheaton's Reports, page* 122.

XXXVII. THORNDIKE *vs.* THE UNITED STATES. (*Page* 64.)

Treasury notes issued under the Act of Congress of 1814, ch. 77 and ch. 699, being by their terms receivable in payment of duties, taxes, and land debts, due to the United States, for the principal and interest thereon, are a good tender, and may be pleaded as such to such debts. These treasury notes are on their face payable in one year with interest up to the day when due, but if not then paid by the government, the interest does not stop, but continues until paid, and may be required by the holder in the same manner as interest might be claimed on a private contract of a like nature.—(THORNDIKE, *in error, vs.* THE UNITED STATES, 2 *Mason's Reports, page* 1.)

XXXVIII. THOMPSON *vs.* RIGGS. (*Page* 74.)

The eighth section of the act of Congress of 1863 (12 *Statutes at Large,* 764), to re-organize the courts of the District of Columbia, and which says, "that if, upon the trial of the cause, an exception be taken, the bill containing it need not be sealed or signed," does not dispense with a regular bill of exceptions in the way usual in circuit courts of the United States when the rulings of the court, in admitting or rejecting evidence, or in giving or refusing instructions, are meant to be brought from the supreme court of the district to *this* court for review. The provision has reference to carrying such rulings from the special to the general term of the supreme court of the district itself. A customer of certain bankers at Washington, D. C., in times when, specie payments having been lately suspended, coin was acquiring one value, and currency (paper money) another and less, deposited with them both coin and paper money; the different deposits being entered in his pass-book, the one as "coin," the other as "currency," &c. Debts being at this time payable by law only in coin, the bankers requested their customer to make his full balance coin, which he did. Congress passed, about eight months afterwards, an act making certain treasury notes lawful money for the payment of debts. The depositor went on depositing "coin" and "treasury notes," then regarded as currency, and both were entered accordingly. He afterwards drew for "coin," for a part of his deposit, exceeding the coin deposited *after* the legal-tender act, and his check was paid in coin. He afterwards drew for "coin,"—the bulk of the coin balance deposited *before* the legal-tender act. Coin was refused and tender made of the notes declared by Congress a legal tender. On suit brought to recover the market value of the coin drawn for,—the bank teller having testified, among other things, that "after the suspension, and particularly after the act making treasury notes a legal tender, his employers uniformly made with customers depositing with them a difference, in receiving and paying their deposits, between coin or specie and paper money, and in all cases when the deposit was in coin they paid the checks of their customers in coin when they called for coin, otherwise they paid currency, treasury or bank notes,"—the plaintiff offered evidence to show "that the usage and mode of dealing between the said parties as set out in the testimony of the teller was uniformly used and practiced by all the banks and bankers of the district of Columbia with their customers.—(THOMPSON *vs.* RIGGS, 5 *Wallace's Reports, page* 663.)

XXXIX. THE UNITED STATES *vs.* MARIGOLD.
(*Pages* 14, 19, 48, 69, 97.)

On the 3d of March, 1825, Congress passed an act (4 *Statutes at Large,* 121) providing for the punishment of persons who shall bring into the United States, with intent to pass, any false, forged, or counterfeit coin, and also for the punishment of those who shall pass, utter, publish, or sell any such false, forged, or counterfeit coin. Congress had the constitutional power to pass this law. Under the power to regulate commerce, Congress can exclude, either partially or wholly, any subject falling within the legitimate sphere of commercial regulations, and under the power to coin money and regulate the value thereof, Congress can protect the creature and object of that power. (THE UNITED STATES *vs.* MARIGOLD, 9 *Howard's U. S. Supreme Court Reports, page* 560.)

XL. VEAZIE BANK *vs.* FENNO. (*Pages* 18, 40, 41.)

The 9th section of the act of July 13, 1866, amendatory of prior internal revenue acts, and which provides that every national banking association, State bank, or State banking association, shall pay a tax of ten per centum on the amounts of the notes of any State bank, or State banking association, paid out by them after the 1st day of August, 1866, does not lay a direct tax within the meaning of that clause of the Constitution which ordains that "direct taxes shall be apportioned among the several States, according to their respective numbers." Congress having undertaken, in the exercise of undisputed constitutional power, to provide a currency for the whole country, may constitutionally secure the benefit of it to the people by appropriate legislation, and to that end may restrain, by suitable enactments, the circulation of any notes, not issued under its own authority. The tax of ten per centum imposed by the act of July 13th, 1866, on the notes of State banks paid out after the first of August, 1866, is warranted by the Constitution.—(VEAZIE BANK *vs.* FENNO, 8 *Wallace's Report, page* 533.)

XLI. WARD *vs.* STATE OF MARYLAND. (*Page* 66.)

A State statute that imposes a discriminating license tax is unconstitutional. A State cannot discriminate in favor of its own citizens. —(WARD *vs.* STATE OF MARYLAND, *American Law Times Reports, January number,* 1872.)

XLII. WASHINGTON BRIDGE CO. *vs.* STEWART. (*Page* 60.)

After a case has been decided upon its merits, and remanded to the court below, if it is again brought up on a second appeal, it is then too late to allege that the court had not jurisdiction to try the first appeal. The Supreme Court has no power to review its decisions, whether in a case at law or equity. A final decree in chancery is as conclusive as a judgment at law. An affirmance by a divided court, either upon a writ of error or appeal, is conclusive upon the rights of the parties. —(WASHINGTON BRIDGE CO. *vs.* STEWART ET AL., 3 *Howard's U. S. Reports, page* 413.)

XLIII. WORKMAN *vs.* MIFFLIN. (*Page* 22.)

A ground rent is not apportioned by the taking of a part of the lot, out of which it is reserved, for a public highway. A ground landlord is not an owner to whom damages can be awarded for the opening of a street through the land. His only remedy is in equity, to have a portion of the damages impounded to meet the accruing rents. If the owners of the land receive the damages awarded, they cannot set up the taking of the land, as a defence to the payment of the ground rent.—(WORKMAN ET AL. *vs.* MIFFLIN. 30 *Pennsylvania Reports, page* 362.

XLIV. WILLARD *vs.* TAYLOE. (*Page* 74.)

A covenant in a lease giving to the lessee a right or option to purchase the premises leased at any time during the term, is in the nature of a continuing offer to sell. The offer thus made, if under seal, is regarded as made upon sufficient consideration, and therefore, one from which the lessor is not at liberty to recede. When accepted by the lessee, a contract of sale is completed. When a contract for the sale of real property is plain and certain in its terms and in its nature, and the circumstances attending its execution are free from objection, it is the usual practice of courts of equity to enforce its specific execution upon the application of the party who has complied with its stipulations on his part, or has reasonably and in good faith offered, and continues ready to comply with them. But it is not the invariable practice. This form of relief is not a matter of absolute right to either party, but a matter resting in the discretion of the court, to be exercised upon a consideration of all the circumstances of each particular case. In general the specific relief will be granted when it is apparent, from a view of all the circumstances of the particular case, that it will subserve the ends of justice; and it will be withheld when, from a like view, it appears that it will produce hardship or injustice to either of the parties. Where specific execution which would work hardship when unconditionally performed, would work equity when decreed on conditions, it will be decreed conditionally. The kind of currency which a party offers in payment of a contract (which, in this case consisted of notes of the United States, not equivalent at the time to gold or silver,) is important, on a bill for specific performance, only in considering the good faith of his conduct.

The condition of the currency in April, 1864, and the general use of notes of the United States at that time, repel any imputation of bad faith in tendering such notes instead of coin in satisfaction of a contract. Where a party is entitled to specific performance of a contract upon the payment of certain sums, and there is uncertainty as to the amount of such sums, he may apply by bill for such specific performance, and submit to the court the question of amount which he should pay. Fluctuations in the value of property contracted for between the date of the contract and the time when execution of the contract is demanded; where the contract was, when made, a fair one, and in its attendant circumstances unobjectionable, are not allowed to prevent a specific enforcement of the contract. The general rule is that the parties to the contract are the only proper parties to the suit for its performance. Hence the assignment by the complainant, prior to his bill, of a partial interest in the entire contract, is no defence to the bill for such performance. Where a party, prior to filing a bill for specific performance

contract for the sale of land, had sent to the other side for exam-
ion, and in professed purpose of execution of the contract, the draft
mortgage which he is ready, on a conveyance being made, to exe-
, it is no defence to the bill, if the defendant have wholly refused to
cute a deed, that the draft is not in such a form as respected parties
the term of years which the security had to run, as the vendor was
nd to accept; especially where such vendor, in returning the draft,
not stated in what particulars he was dissatisfied with the draft.
en parties have reduced their contract to writing, conversations con-
ling or changing their stipulations are, in the absence of fraud, no
re received in a court of equity than in a court of law. In this case,
hout expressing an opinion upon the constitutionality of the pro-
ion of the act of Congress which makes U. S. notes a legal tender for
vate debts, nor whether, if constitutional, the provision is to be limit-
in its application to contracts made subsequent to the passage of the
, the court refused to decree a conveyance of real estate, on the tender
such notes, where the estate had greatly risen in value, where at the
e of the contract gold and silver coin were the only lawful money
the United States, and where it was impossible to suppose that the
rties when making their contract—which was eight years before the
tes were authorized—contemplated a substitution of such notes
hen tendered much depreciated) for coin; but did decree a specific
ecution, upon the payment in coin of the price originally agreed on,
th interest in coin also.—(WILLARD *vs.* TAYLOE, 8 *Wallace's Reports*,
ge 557.)

XLV. WRIGHT *vs.* REID. (*Page* 74.)

Bank notes are money within the annuity act.—(17 *George, page* 111,
apter 26. WRIGHT *vs.* REID, 3 *Term Reports, page* 554.)

NATIONAL BANK ACT.

EDITION OF 1872.

CONTENTS.

		PAGE
I. 1864. June 3.	The National Bank Act.............................	11
II. 1865. April 6.	Amendment of the National Bank Act............	28
III. 1865. March 3.	Amendment of the Bank Act...................	29
IV. 1867. March 2.	An Act to provide Ways and Means for the payment of Compound Interest Notes.......................	30
V. 1868. February 10.	An Act in relation to taxing shares in National Banks...	30
VI. 1868. July 25.	An Act to provide for a further issue of temporary Loan Certificates..	31
VII. 1869. February 19.	An Act to prevent loaning money upon United States Notes...	31
VIII. 1869. March 3.	An Act regulating the Reports of National Banking Associations.....................................	32
IX. 1869. March 3.	An Act in reference to certifying Checks on National Banks...	33
X. 1869. April 6.	Amendment of National Bank Act................	33
XI. 1870. July 8.	Amendment of National Bank Act................	33
XII. 1870. July 12.	An Act to provide for the redemption of the Three per Cent. Temporary Loan Certificates, and for an increase of National Bank Notes..	34
XIII. 1870. July 14.	An Act to require National Banks, going into liquidation, to retire their Circulating Notes...................	37
XIV. 1866. July 13.	An Act in relation to taxation of State Bank Notes; etc..	37
XV. 1864. June 30.	An Act in relation to Monthly Tax on Deposits...	39
XVI. 1867. March 2.	An Act in relation to refunding of overpayments by National Banks	40
XVII.	Decisions of the Supreme Court of the United States and of the State Courts, and of the Comptroller of the Currency and the Commissioner of Internal Revenue, in relation to the National Bank Act..	45

CONTENTS—*continued.*

DECISIONS.— PAGE
1. Organization of a National Bank 45
2. Evidence of Organization 46
3. Bank Notes 47
4. Redemption of National Bank Notes 48
5. Limit of Liabilities 50
6. Usury and its Defenses 51, 81
7. Lawful Money Reserve 52
8. Loans on Bank Shares 55
9. Taxation by States and by the U. S. 55
10. Construction of the word "PLACE," 62
11. National Banks as Fiscal Agents of the U. S. 64
12. National Banks as State Agents for the collection of State Tax on Shares 64
13. Taxation of Circulation of State Banks 66
14. State Banks—their Liability under the Act of Congress 67
15. Depositary Banks—Treasury Decisions 72
16. Failure to Redeem Circulation 74
17. Offences by National Bank Officers 76
18. Suits under the National Bank Act 78
19. Miscellaneous 79
20. Certification of Bank Checks 80

XVIII.—TREASURY DECISIONS 81
1. Usury by National Banks 82
2. Bank Returns 82
3. Taxation of Bank Shares 83
4. Semi-Annual Returns and Payment of Taxes 84
5. Depositary National Banks 92
6. Failure of a National Bank 92
7. Tax on Notes of State Banks 93
8. Internal Revenue Duties 93

XIX.—INTERNAL REVENUE LAW.
1. Tax on Bank Dividends 97
2. Return of Dividends 98
3. Tax on Brokers, Banks and Bankers 98
4. Tax on Deposits, Capital Stock and Circulation 99

XX.—DECISION OF THE SUPREME COURT, U. S., February, 1871, in the case of the Merchants' National Bank, Boston, *vs.* the State National Bank 101

XXI.—GENERAL INDEX.

THE NATIONAL BANK ACT.

The National Bank Act of June, 1864, with the Amendments of 1865–1870, to which are added the decisions of the Supreme Court of the United States, and of the State Courts; and decisions and rulings of the Comptroller of the Currency, and the Commissioner of Internal Revenue, in reference to said Act, from 1865 to 1870. This is the first and only edition comprising the entire Act, and the numerous decisions in reference thereto, together with the name of the redemption agent of each Bank.

NEW YORK, 1871: PUBLISHED AT THE
OFFICE OF THE BANKERS' MAGAZINE AND STATISTICAL REGISTER,
No. 23 Murray Street.

Price Two Dollars.

- "'THE LIVING AGE' has no equal in any country." — *From the Press, Philadelphia.*
- "The best of all our eclectic publications." — *From the Nation, New York.*
- "It stands at the head of nineteenth-century literature." — *From the Evening Journal, Chicago.*
- "The best periodical in America." — *From Rev. Theo. L. Cuyler.*

LITTELL'S LIVING AGE,

Of which more than *One Hundred Volumes* have been published, has received the commendation of the most eminent men of the country; and it admittedly "continues to stand at the head of its class."

IT IS ISSUED EVERY SATURDAY, giving fifty-two numbers, of sixty-four pages each, or more than Three Thousand double-column octavo pages of reading-matter yearly; enabling it to present with a combined freshness and completeness nowhere else attempted,

The best Essays, Reviews, Criticisms, Serial and Short Stories, Poetry, Scientific, Biographical, Historical, and Political Information, gathered from the entire body of Foreign Periodical Literature.

The ablest and most cultured intellects in every department of Literature, Politics, Science, and Art, find expression in the Periodical Literature of Europe, and especially of Great Britain.

The Living Age, forming four large volumes a year, furnishes, from the vast and generally inaccessible mass of this literature, the only compilation that, while within the reach of all, is satisfactory in the COMPLETENESS with which it embraces whatever is of immediate interest, or of solid, permanent value.

It is therefore **indispensable** to every one who wishes to keep pace with the events or intellectual progress of the time, or to cultivate in himself or his family general intelligence and literary taste.

Extracts from Recent Notices.

From Rev. Henry Ward Beecher.
"Were I, in view of all the competitors that are now in the field, to choose, I should certainly choose 'THE LIVING AGE.' . . . Nor is there in any library that I know of, so much instructive and entertaining reading in the same number of volumes."

From the Congregationalist, Boston.
"None of the eclectics can be matched with this as to substantial value and interest."

From the New-York Evening Post.
"The editors permit nothing good in the whole range of the European magazines and reviews to escape them. . . . In no other single publication can there be found so much of sterling literary excellence."

From the Boston Post.
"It gives to its readers more than three thousand double-column octavo pages a year, of the most valuable, instructive, and entertaining reading of the day. 'History, biography, fiction, poetry, wit, science, politics, criticism, art,—what is not here?' It is the only compilation that presents with a satisfactory completeness, as well as freshness, the best literature of the almost innumerable, and generally inaccessible, European quarterlies, monthlies, and weeklies,—a literature embracing the productions of the ablest and most cultured writers living."

From the Williams Quarterly.
"It is inexhaustible. It has as much that is good as a dozen ordinary magazines combined."

From the Advance, Chicago.
"For thinking people, the best of all the eclectic publications, and *the cheapest*. . . . It is a monthly that *comes every week.*"

From the Lutheran and Missionary, Phila.
"An extraordinary value marks many of the articles of this publication, because they are the productions of the ablest men of our times."

From the Philadelphia Evening Bulletin.
"The most admirable thesaurus of current reading now collected in any country."

From the Illinois State Journal.
"It has more real solid worth, more useful information, than any similar publication we know of. The ablest essays, the most entertaining stories, the finest poetry, of the English language, are here gathered together."

From the Milwaukie Daily Sentinel.
"More than ever indispensable, in these days of frequent publication in expensive English reviews, of articles on the great questions of current inquiry, by such men as Max Muller, Huxley, Tyndall, and many others."

From the Mobile Daily Register.
"Still peerless among periodicals in value to the reader."

From the Pacific, San Francisco.
"Its publication in weekly numbers gives to it a great advantage over its monthly contemporaries in the spirit and freshness of its contents."

From the Chicago Daily Republican.
"It occupies a field filled by no other periodical. The subscriber to 'LITTELL' finds himself in possession at the end of the year, of four large volumes of *such reading as can be obtained in no other form*, and comprising selections from every department of science, art, philosophy, and *belles-lettres*. Those who desire a THOROUGH COMPENDIUM of all that is admirable and noteworthy in the literary world will be spared the trouble of wading through the sea of reviews and magazines published abroad; for they will find the essence of all compacted and concentrated here."

From the Christian Examiner, Richmond.
"The great eclectic of this country."

Published weekly at $8,00 a year, *free of postage.* An extra copy sent gratis to any one getting up a Club of five New Subscribers. Address

LITTELL & GAY, 30 Bromfield Street, Boston.

THE BEST HOME AND FOREIGN LITERATURE AT CLUB PRICES.

["Possessed of 'LITTELL'S LIVING AGE' and of one or other of our vivacious American monthlies, a subscriber will find himself in command of the whole situation." — *Philadelphia Evening Bulletin.*"]

For *Ten Dollars*, THE LIVING AGE, weekly, containing the cream of Foreign Periodical Literature, and either one of the leading magazines of Home Literature named below, will be sent to one address for one year; viz.,—

HARPER'S MONTHLY (or WEEKLY or BAZAR), THE ATLANTIC MONTHLY, LIPPINCOTT'S MONTHLY, THE GALAXY, OLD AND NEW, THE OVERLAND MONTHLY, or APPLETON'S JOURNAL (weekly); or, for $8.50, THE LIVING AGE and OUR YOUNG FOLKS. Address as above.

THE PREMIUM ON GOLD.

A VALUABLE BOOK FOR BANKERS AND BROKERS.

TOWERS' *Premium Tables for Buying and Selling Gold, Bonds and Stocks. Giving the premium on any amount from one dollar to ten thousand dollars, from one-eighth of one per cent. to twenty-five and seven-eighths per cent. Price three dollars.*

These tables are admirably adapted for use by bankers and brokers. For instance, by turning to page marked 11 per cent. we find the premium on $19 in gold at $11\frac{7}{8}$ per cent. to be 2.25\frac{5}{8}$, or for $190, by adding the cipher, we have $22.56; or if we want to sell a $5,000 bond at $13\frac{5}{8}$ per cent. premium, we have $5,681.25-100 as the result.

It also gives the discount from par to $74\frac{1}{4}$ per cent. by one-eighth per cent. And if the interest is required on $400 for one year at $9\frac{1}{2}$ per cent. per annum, we have $38, or for 60 days one-sixth of $38.

The publishers have received high commendations from New York Banks and others, which is proven by their not only using one copy but purchasing extra copies for several clerks.

Among the Banks who are now using "TOWERS' PREMIUM TABLES" are the following:

NEW-YORK.

American Exchange Nat'l Bank,	Stuyvesant Bank,
Merchants' Exchange Nat'l Bank,	Bowery Savings Bank,
Shoe and Leather Nat'l Bank,	Nassau Bank,
Union Square Nat'l Bank,	Seamans' Savings Bank,
National Bank of Commerce,	Manhattan Savings Bank,
Commonwealth National Bank,	National Park Bank,
St. Nicholas National Bank,	Union Dime Savings Bank.

BROOKLYN.

Williamsburg Savings Bank,   The Fulton Bank.

BOSTON.

City National Bank,	Mercantile Savings Institution,
Columbian National Bank,	Bowles Brothers & Co.,
Globe National Bank,	B. W. Gilbert.

PHILADELPHIA.

Commonwealth National Bank,   Painter & Co., Bankers.

BALTIMORE.

Brown, Lancaster & Co.

One Volume, Quarto.   Price Three Dollars.

NEW YORK:
PUBLISHED AT THE OFFICE OF THE BANKERS' MAGAZINE.
1871.